*Dean*

# GOD'S DIVINE APPOINTMENTS:

## BRINGING GLORY TO HIM THROUGH THEM

BY

DEAN C. TRUNE

Dean Trune
4642 Arrowhead Road
Okemos, Michigan 48864
or
www.deantrune.com
dtrune@gmail.com

ISBN 978-0-9837865-0-4

Cover Design by Natalie Pennington

Photo on rear cover by Jackie Palmer

Printed in USA by Malloy Press

Unless otherwise identified, all Bible quotations are taken
from the New International Version®. NIV®. Copyright©
1973, 1978, 1984 by International Bible Society.

The stories on pages 23, and 175 are taken from *The Path Toward Passion* (PrayerShop Publishing © 2009). They are used
by permission.

# ACKNOWLEDGMENTS

I utilized the services of two incredible editors for this book. In addition to being editors, they are friends. They did a phenomenal job. Allow me to introduce you to both of them.

**Gale Juhl:** He is an attorney living in Pleasant Hill, Iowa. He is a dear friend. I would say of him the same thing that Paul said in Philippians 2:25 of Epaphroditus, "my brother, co-worker, and fellow soldier." He has blessed congregations and organizations with his leadership. He has blessed many congregations in transition as an interim minister. I know of no one like him. He has been a blessing to me and to my family in more ways than I can count.

**Joy Baade:** Bonnie and I count her as a dear friend. She attends the same church that we do, the South Lansing Christian Church in Lansing, Michigan. Even though she has no physical sight, she has been blessed with abundant insight and wisdom. Her command of the English language is extremely impressive. She excels in everything she does. She coordinates various ministries at SLCC and is a friend to multitudes. We are blessed to be able to call her our friend.

God used both of them to greatly improve the readability of this book. We are all blessed by their editing abilities. I shudder to think what this book would be without their expertise. Thank you, Gale and Joy!

# TABLE OF CONTENTS

# INTRODUCTION

**M**y first book, *The Path Toward Passion*, discussed ways that we can intentionally spend time with God Himself. We often choose to spend our time in activities with people rather than with God. Typically, our time with God will lead us into activities with people. If our time with God brings Him glory, then our activities with people will also bring Him glory. I realize that might be an oversimplification, but our primary aim with this one life that He has given us is to glorify Him.

The same is true of God's divine appointments. He desires to be glorified through the divine appointments that He orchestrates for us. It is not about our technique or our abilities but simply about glorifying Him. I believe that the more divine appointments that I recognize and allow Him to use me, the greater the glory He will receive.

So there appears to be a pattern developing in my writing.

1st book: *The Path Toward Passion*–
   **glorifying God** in our pursuit of Him.

2nd book: *God's Divine Appointments*–
   **glorifying God** in divine appointments.

3rd book (someday): *Radical Character*–
   **glorifying God** in our character.

I believe that the best way to introduce this book on God's divine appointments is to honestly ask myself five powerful questions.

1. How many divine appointments did I miss last week or even today?

11

2. What was God attempting to teach me in the divine appointment that I missed?

3. What sort of heart moving worship of Him have I missed because I didn't recognize a divine appointment that He orchestrated just for me?

4. Who "missed out" on God's love today because I was completely absorbed with myself?

5. How often do I miss God's affirmation of my obedience because I either miss a divine appointment or misinterpret one?

Powerful questions make me think. I purpose not to cheat God out of the glory due Him in the divine appointments He orchestrates for me. There are far too many consequences for myself and others when divine appointments are missed. I shudder when I think of all the opportunities I have missed.

The first five chapters of this book discuss the concept of divine appointments. The next 58 chapters contain stories of divine appointments that God has orchestrated for me and for others. Following each story, I have listed a principle that this particular divine appointment illustrates. God is exceptional at drawing us to His truth through divine appointments.

*"Holy God, help us to live in your Presence and be powerfully aware of what You are orchestrating in us and through us. It is far too important to miss! May You be glorified in majestic ways through the divine appointments You bring into our lives."*

# CHAPTER 1

# WHAT IS A DIVINE APPOINTMENT?

The purpose of this book is to encourage you to be on the lookout for the divine appointments that God orchestrates in your life and to intentionally pursue being a blessing in people's lives through divine appointments. We miss far too many of them.

*"Be wise in the way you act toward outsiders; make the most of every opportunity." Colossians 4:5*

Paul tells us that wisdom and intentionality are required to make a difference in encounters with people.

*A divine appointment is a God-arranged event connected with a person. It includes both a person and an event. You cannot have a divine appointment without a person, and you cannot have a divine appointment without an event to connect you to a person.*

In order to "see" divine appointments from God's perspective, I must initially believe that God has the <u>ability</u> and that God has the <u>desire</u> to give us divine appointments. I believe that He does. He is an amazing God!

I have discovered divine appointments with people who are:

- waiting on my table in a restaurant
- sitting next to me on an airplane
- standing next to me in a line
- participating at automobile accidents

- sharing a table at a conference or seminar
- jogging around my neighborhood
- sitting next to me somewhere
- sitting in a public area
- dialing my phone by mistake
- checking me out of a store
- serving as flight attendants
- walking up to me in my yard
- renting me a car
- trying to sell me something
- attempting to convince me to join their cult
- repairing something in my house
- asking for directions
- visiting my garage sale
- visiting someone else's garage sale
- and a variety of other situations

I have had divine appointments with people who were:

- passionate Christians
- nominal Christians
- pagans
- Muslims
- Jehovah Witnesses
- Mormons
- atheists
- Jews
- happy people
- angry people
- hurting people
- fearful people
- anxious people
- chatty people
- quiet people
- clueless people

- delightful people
- crying people
- famous people

What have I done with divine appointments?

- asked for a prayer request  (99.9% of the time)
- gave my business card to them (15%-20% of the time)
- prayed with him/her right then  (a few occasions)
- gave my Bible away  (a few occasions)
- bought lunch  (a few occasions)
- gave my first book to them  (a few occasions)

I firmly believe that having divine appointments is one of the most enjoyable and deeply rewarding activities we can experience as Christians. It is exciting to see God at work in His mission of blessing and reaching the world with His love and truth.

Asking the right question is important in obtaining a prayer request from a divine appointment. Most of the time I ask one of the following questions:

A. *"I always look for something in the lives of people that I meet that I can pray about for the next month. Is there something in your life that I can be praying for you?"*

B. *"We always look for something in our waitress's or waiter's life that we can pray about over the next month. Could you give it some thought and let us know before we leave? We would be happy to pray?"*

15

*C. "God did this on purpose. What can I be praying for you?"*

Here are some things that I need to remember when encountering divine appointments:

1. *"But the LORD said to Samuel, 'Do not consider his appearance or his height, for I have rejected him. The LORD does not look at the things people look at. People look at the outward appearance, but the LORD looks at the heart.'"*
I Samuel 16:7

We see the outside. God sees the heart. Sometimes I will walk away from a divine appointment, and I will tell God, "That wasn't much." God often reminds me that He sees the heart, and I need to be praying for that person.

2. Many people have deep hurts but do not have someone that cares enough to pray. Some people live and work in a place far from friends and relatives. If they are not connected with others outside of work, they may have a need but no one to talk with face to face. Some of my divine appointments just simply needed to have a conversation with someone face to face. I am surprised how quickly strangers will open up when they sense that they can trust us. I certainly believe that God wants to work supernaturally through us.

3. I have heard it said that non-Christians often need about seven encouraging encounters with Jesus (through His children) before they are ready to receive Him. Certainly this is not an exact science. You and I need to help people just simply find their next step on their spiritual journey. It seems that sometimes I have been their first encounter with Jesus, and sometimes I have met people who are ready to say

"yes" to Him. I want to be a person God uses to move people along on their spiritual journey.

4. *"Live such good lives among the pagans that, though they accuse you of doing wrong, they may see your good deeds and glorify God on the day he visits us."* I Peter 2:12

*"Let your conversation be always full of grace, seasoned with salt, so that you may know how to answer everyone."* Colossians 4:6

I must remember to be respectful and tactful with divine appointments. I have often encountered people who were so rudely treated by Christians in the past that they did not even want to have a conversation with me. Instead of being recognized as Jesus' disciples because of our love for one another (John 13:35), we become known for our arrogance, judgmentalism, and meanness. Love people but hate sin. How hard is that for us to figure out?

5. *"Be very careful, then, how you live—not as unwise but as wise, making the most of every opportunity, because the days are evil."* Ephesians 5:15-16

I need to quietly listen to God, look for opportunities, and ask the right questions. Our God gives wisdom to those who ask (James 1:5). The right answer does not make people think. But when you and I ask the right questions, people have to pause and reflect. The right answer is knowledge. The right question is wisdom.

6. *"Now to him who is able to do immeasurably more than all we ask or imagine, according to his power that is at work within us, to him be glory in the church and in Christ Jesus*

*throughout all generations, for ever and ever! Amen."*
Ephesians 3:20-21

I need to constantly expect God to do the unexpected. Our God is incredible at working "outside of our expectations." He not only thinks outside the box; He doesn't even have a box that limits Him. God has so impressed me at times with His exact timing or His words of wisdom that I am simply in awe of His greatness. Some of the stories that I share in this book will amaze you just as I have been amazed.

7. *"Be self-controlled and alert. Your enemy the devil prowls around like a roaring lion looking for someone to devour."* I Peter 5:8

Satan hates for us to have divine appointments in ways where God is glorified. He hates it when we join Jesus in His mission to bless and reach people. Naturally we need to expect Satan to resist us by tempting us with fear or apathy toward people. People can be intimidating. It is easy not to love people. It is easy to walk right past opportunities and focus on ourselves. Satan tempts us with this all the time. I must remember that when I fear others or when I just don't care about blessing and loving people, I am joining Satan and his mission. I refuse to do that. We are at war. I can't allow myself to be taken out of the conflict by my self-centeredness.

CHAPTER 2

# WHY A BOOK ON DIVINE APPOINTMENTS?

Most Christians talk about divine appointments. Many Christians have regularly experienced divine appointments. So why do we need a book written on divine appointments? I can think of three solid reasons.

**1. To "See" God at Work:** As with most Christians throughout history, we become more excited about loving and serving God when we have a "front row seat" to what He is doing. Seeing God at work, close up, reminds us that we serve a phenomenal, all-powerful God who desires to use us mightily in His Kingdom. Some twenty-first century Christians think that we have a God who needs to be defended, who is incapable of handling our issues, and who, at best, is weak and unresponsive. They may not articulate these thoughts out loud, but they live life as if these perspectives were absolutely true.

One verse that stirs my heart is John 5:17:

*"Jesus said to them, 'My Father is always at his work to this very day, and I too, am working.'"*

When we Christians pray self-centeredly, live self-servingly, and pursue God half-heartedly, it is difficult to "see" God at work. He has prescribed heart surgery to remove the pride that leads to self-dependence, self-exaltation, and self-love. Instead, He desires surrender, humility, and passion for Him on our part. Jesus perfectly demonstrated these qualities, and we need to simply follow in His steps. A divine appointment is one way that God allows us to see Him at work. It is not the only way, but it is one way.

**2. I Miss Too Many Divine Appointments:** Even though we know about divine appointments, many of us Christians miss the vast majority of the divine appointments that God provides. Often God is cheated out of glory for Himself because we even miss those that are extremely obvious. Personally, I am constantly looking for divine appointments, but I still can be distracted into missing many golden opportunities to glorify Him. For Christians not looking for divine appointments, my guess is that they miss at least two-thirds of what God is doing. I have no idea of the exact percentage; I just know that it is too high. Quite possibly a book on divine appointments may help people recognize more of them before the moment has passed.

**3. Understanding God's Reasons for Divine Appointments:** I believe that many of us recognize divine appointments when they occur, but we do not have a perspective on what God is attempting to accomplish through these appointments. God provides divine appointments for many reasons, including the following:

> A. Intercession: He wants us to be praying for others.

> B. Salvation: He is looking for people who will introduce others to Him.

> C. Reminders: He desires us to constantly remember who He really is.

> D. Teaching: He is always attempting to refine our characters; often divine

appointments are primarily for us, not for others. We need help in seeing His perspective on us and our development as His disciples.

Throughout this book, you will find information on divine appointments and examples of God at work in the midst of divine appointments. Recognizing His divine appointments often requires humility, sometimes boldness, and always love. I do not want to miss anything that He is doing or attempting to accomplish. Life is too short to miss *God's Divine Appointments*.

*"Holy Father, Open our eyes!"*

# CHAPTER 3

# GOD GETS ME STARTED WITH DIVINE APPOINTMENTS

This is a story that first appeared in my book, *The Path Toward Passion,* Prayershop Publishing 2009.

It is the summer of 1986, and my family and I are returning to East Lansing, Michigan, from the Battle Creek International Balloon Championship. We are driving up I-69 toward Lansing when the driver's side rear tire goes flat on our 1981 Toyota Celica.

I am convinced that God does not give us flat tires to "test" our ability to change tires. He typically gives us flat tires for building character and/or for divine appointments. I am just plain annoyed at this flat tire.

I get everyone out of the car and begin removing the tire changing equipment from the trunk. Much to my surprise, I cannot find a lug nut wrench anywhere in the car. We have owned the car for a few months, but I have never checked to determine if I have everything I need to change a tire.

Plan A is to wait for someone to stop and help us. No one stops.

Plan B is to make a sign that says, "Need Lug Nut Wrench." I give it to my son, Ryan, (he is nine years old) and he stands behind the car facing oncoming traffic. No one stops.

23

Finally we go to Plan C. We decide we need to do something else because it will be getting dark in about an hour. We determine that Ryan and I will walk to the next expressway exit and try to find a lug nut wrench. Bonnie and our daughter, Kim, will wait in the car.

Ryan and I have walked less than a hundred yards when a car stops to help. We run back to our car. A young man in a big Chevy Impala asks if we need help. I explain to him that we need a lug nut wrench to change the tire. He retrieves his lug nut wrench from his trunk and encourages me to try it; it works. This young man talks with Ryan and me while I change the tire. When I am finished, I give him back his lug nut wrench, and he leaves.

As we are driving home, my son, with his nine-year-old wisdom, says, "Dad, I am little disappointed." I ask, "Why?" He replies, "You didn't find out if he is a Christian." All of a sudden it hits me. This kind young man was a divine appointment. The reason no one else stopped is that God wanted us to encourage him. My son teaches me much about divine appointments this day. I need to be aware of the divine appointments that God orchestrates.

A few years later, I am driving to Northern Michigan University in Marquette, Michigan. I am filling in for the campus minister, who is not able to attend the fellowship meeting tonight. I am driving across Highway 2, which is just a two-lane road. If you have ever been to the upper peninsula of Michigan, you already know that not very many people live there. There are mainly trees and animals.

I come up over a ridge, and there is a van attached to a pop-up camper parked off to the side of the road. As I speed by, God prompts me to stop, so I turn around and pull up

24

across the road from the people standing by the van. I roll down my window and ask if they need help.

The husband says, "We need a lug nut wrench." I just start grinning. I ask if the lug nut wrench is needed for the van or the pop-up. He replies, "The pop-up."

I grab the lug nut wrench from my car and head across the road. The man tries it on the pop-up, and it works. These lug nut wrenches must be universal. I converse with them for a while and commit to pray for them. As I resume my trip to Marquette, I cannot help but laugh. I tell God, "You have such a sense of humor. I can't believe that You gave me a divine appointment with someone who needed a lug nut wrench."

God is trying to make it perfectly clear to me that He arranges divine appointments. It will be another few years before I begin keeping a divine appointment journal and praying regularly for my divine appointments. Divine appointments do not happen by chance. We serve an amazing God Who orchestrates them. I do not want to miss even one.

CHAPTER 4

# LEVELS OF AWARENESS OF DIVINE APPOINTMENTS

**W**hy is it that some Christians are very aware of divine appointments, and some Christians never "see" one? I believe that it has much to do with living in the presence of God. If we are living in the reality of His presence, then we will recognize what He is doing when He brings people across our path. All of us fit into one of the following levels of awareness concerning divine appointments:

**1. Complete Unawareness:** Christians at this level do not see the presence of people or the presence of God woven into their activities. In fact, the activities themselves are more important than the people involved in the activities. For example, there is a greater focus on me being served a meal in a restaurant than on the people serving me. Also, when I am flying, there is a greater focus on me reaching a destination than on who is sitting beside me. Self often blinds me to the recognition of divine appointments. As we covered in the last chapter, "self" usually shows up as:

> A. fear of people
> B. apathy toward people
>    (both involve ignoring the Holy Spirit's
>       promptings)

**2. Partial Awareness:** Christians at this level see the presence of people and the presence of God only when both are very obvious. Typically, there are:
> A. no assumptions that God is at work

    B. no questions to determine where God is at
       work
    C. no acts of caring or interest in the people
       themselves

**3. Full Awareness:** Christians at this level are constantly aware of the presence of people and the presence of God in most, if not all, situations and events. They are expecting and watching for God to show up and glorify Himself.

I firmly believe that even though we aim for **Full Awareness**, we sometimes miss the divine appointment because we temporarily become caught up in the activity or event, and we cease to see God at work. I have missed some potentially great divine appointments because I am thinking only of the activity, or I am being disobedient, or I am focused only on my needs. It happens. When it occurs, I just need to repent and move on with greater awareness of my God at work. I really do want to see what God sees and hear what God hears.

Psalm 139:16 in the New Living Translation speaks with great certainty of God's awareness of me.

*"You saw me before I was born.*
*Every day of my life was recorded in your book.*
*Every moment was laid out before a single day had*
*passed."*

May I be as aware of Him.

# CHAPTER 5

# DIVINE APPOINTMENTS IN SCRIPTURE

The Bible is full of occasions where God orchestrated a divine appointment between two or more people. Each one has a specific purpose, and each one is consistent with His overall plan. Once again, Jesus said in John 5:17, *"My Father is always at his work..."* Divine appointments are demonstrations of His work. Here are some of my favorites.

**1. Abraham's servant meeting Rebekah in the town of Nahor in Genesis 24.**

Abraham sends his chief servant back to Nahor to find a wife for Isaac. Abraham states to his servant that the Lord will send an angel to assist him in finding a wife for Isaac (vs. 7). The servant even sets a condition in his prayer about how he will know who God is providing for Isaac. Rebekah shows up before Abraham's servant is even finished praying. God supernaturally connects them in this divine appointment in order to provide Isaac with a wife of His choosing. God's timing is perfect!

**2. Joseph's brothers' brief encounter with the Ishmaelites who bought Joseph while on their way to Egypt in Genesis 37.**

Joseph's brothers plan to kill him, but Reuben, the oldest, plans to rescue him from the cistern (vs. 21). In Reuben's absence, Joseph's brothers notice a caravan of Ishmaelites headed for Egypt. Judah convinces his brothers (vs. 26) to sell Joseph instead of killing him. Joseph then heads to

Egypt, where thirteen years later he becomes second in command of the whole country. God uses a divine appointment for the sons of Jacob with the Ishmaelites that will save them from the famine over twenty years later. Our God is incredible!

**3. Joseph meeting Pharaoh's cupbearer and baker in prison in Genesis 40.**

Joseph is put in charge of the prison where he is serving time for a crime he did not commit. Pharaoh's chief cupbearer and chief baker are placed in the same prison as Joseph. Joseph accurately predicts their fates, and the chief cupbearer is reinstated to his former position but forgets about Joseph for the next two years. The chief cupbearer eventually tells Pharaoh that Joseph can interpret dreams, and Joseph is promoted to Pharaoh's second in command. We can be in an isolated, character-building place in life, even when we are not at fault, and God can still provide divine appointments that totally change everything. Our God is so good at what He does!

**4. The daughter of Pharaoh finds Moses in the Nile in Exodus 2**

Pharaoh has given the order that every newborn Hebrew boy must be thrown into the Nile. When Moses is born, his parents hide him for three months. When he can no longer be hidden, his parents put him in a little floating ark in the Nile River, and Pharaoh's daughter discovers Moses. Not only is Moses allowed to live, but he is raised in Pharaoh's palace. God is amazing!

**5. Moses meets his future in-laws at a well in Midian in Exodus 2.**

After committing murder, Moses flees to Midian where he sits down by a well. While he is resting from his journey, Jethro's daughters arrive to draw water for their father's sheep. Some shepherds try to drive the women away, but Moses comes to their rescue. He eventually marries one of the women. Again, God's timing is perfect.

**6. Joshua's spies meet Rahab in Joshua 2.**

The children of Israel are finally ready to enter the land that God has promised them. Joshua secretly sends two spies across the Jordan River to spy out the land, including Jericho. Rahab welcomes them into her home and rescues them from the king of Jericho. She deceives the king and helps the spies escape. Rahab and her whole family are spared when the Israelites destroy Jericho. It is an incredible divine appointment for both Rahab's family and the spies.

**7. Samuel meets Saul in I Samuel 9.**

Saul is out looking for his father's donkeys and cannot find them. He and his servant with him decide to ask the prophet Samuel where they can locate the lost donkeys. They ask a person for directions to Samuel's house, and it happens to be Samuel himself. Before Saul leaves that place, Samuel anoints him as Israel's first king. God uses lost donkeys to bring Saul across Samuel's path. God is phenomenal at putting us in the right spot at the right time!

**8. David and Goliath meet in I Samuel 17.**

David is not a part of the army of the Israelites but visits the front lines at his father's request to check on the welfare of his brothers. David quickly assesses the situation, fights Goliath himself, and defeats him. This happens to be one more mighty step for David in becoming Israel's next king. God brings glory to Himself by using someone who will stand up for Him, regardless of the odds.

### 9. Saul enters the exact cave where David is hiding in I Samuel 24.

Saul is chasing David with the intent of killing him. David and his fighting men are hiding in a cave. Saul enters that exact cave, unaware that David and his men are in it. Only God could do this. David has the opportunity to kill Saul but chooses instead to honor the Lord's anointed and show him mercy. God powerfully uses this divine appointment to convict Saul of his mistreatment of David (even though it is a temporary conviction) and for David to demonstrate godly character in the midst of great temptation.

### 10. Obadiah finds Elijah in I Kings 18.

Elijah has told King Ahab that it is not going to rain again until Elijah says so. After three years of no rain, the land is experiencing a severe famine. Ahab blames Elijah and is trying hard to locate him. Ahab and Obadiah, a devout believer in the Lord, scour the land for feed for their animals. Ahab heads in one direction, and Obadiah heads in a different direction. As Obadiah is walking along, Elijah meets him. When God is ready to move supernaturally (as He does on Mt. Carmel), He brings the right people together at the right time to make it happen.

### 11. Jesus meets the Samaritan woman at Jacob's well in John 4.

Jesus is tired from the journey, and this well is a "rest stop" between Judea and Galilee. Jesus does not approach the woman; she comes to Him. This divine appointment brings revival to a town of Samaritans. God is so good!

**12. The two disciples meet the man with a jar on his head, who leads to the place for the last supper in Mark 14.**

Obviously Jesus has told His disciples who to follow in this story of locating where the Passover meal is to be eaten. It is another example of how God orchestrates divine appointments. The disciples are to look for a man carrying a jar of water (an unlikely sight since women mainly carried the water). The house that this man will enter is where the Passover meal will be held.

**13. Simeon meeting Mary and Joseph with Jesus in the temple courts in Luke 2.**

The Spirit tells Simeon that he will not die until he has seen the Messiah. Moved by the Spirit, he goes into the temple courts, where he encounters Joseph and Mary with Jesus (vs. 27). This divine appointment leads to Simeon praising God and prophesying about Jesus' life and ministry.

**14. Jesus has a divine appointment with the repentant thief on the cross in Luke 23.**

God is so good at providing divine appointments for us when we are entirely focused on something else. At a time when Jesus could have been very self-focused, He takes the time to communicate with the two thieves. It is a great lesson for us to remember.

**15.  Andrew meets the boy with five loaves and two fish at the feeding of the five thousand in John 6.**

We do not know where Andrew finds the young lad among the crowd of five thousand plus. Somehow God directs him across Andrew's path in order for the five thousand plus to be fed. Andrew even knows exactly how many small barley loaves and small fish the boy possesses. It is possible that this young lad was the only one with food that day. What an incredible divine appointment.

**16.  Jesus and his disciples encounter the man born blind in John 9.**

Jesus and His disciples are walking along, when they see a man who was born blind. This divine appointment drastically changes this man's life forever when Jesus miraculously  gives him physical sight and spiritual insight. This encounter illustrates how divine appointments can be totally life changing.

**17.  Peter and John meet the crippled man at the temple gate called Beautiful in Acts 3.**

On their way to pray, Peter and John encounter a crippled man who interrupts their intended activity. This reminds us that God will provide divine appointments that seem to be interruptions to our plans. We need to be constantly alert to what God is doing, even if it means changing our plans.

**18.  Philip and the Ethiopian eunuch meet on the desert road in Acts 8.**

Through an angel, God directs Philip to go south to the road that leads from Jerusalem to Gaza. On his way, he encounters the Ethiopian's chariot. Philip understands that God is working, so he runs to the chariot and asks the perfect question. Sometimes we need God's help in knowing what to ask a divine appointment. This conversation took place because Philip responded in obedience to divine direction.

**19. Paul and Silas meet Lydia while looking for a place to pray in Acts 16.**

Paul and Silas (and quite possibly Luke, since he uses the pronoun "we") go outside the city gate expecting to find a place of prayer. Again God interrupts their plans, even to pray, in order to speak to some women about the gospel. We need to pay attention to what God is currently doing and adjust our schedules accordingly.

Typically God orchestrates, and we are to follow. We must constantly be on the alert for divine appointments because we never know when the next one will occur.

# CHAPTER 6

# A WIDE VARIETY OF DIVINE APPOINTMENTS

I am amazed at the wide variety of divine appointments that God orchestrates. I have recorded over 2,200 divine appointments in my journal over the last fourteen years. I normally commit to pray for their prayer requests for a month, and I do. Beyond that, I actually pray for the person for 13 months. I will pray for my divine appointments in December of this year through December of next year.

Here are some of the responses that I have received when I have asked for a prayer request.

- Joyce, a waitress in New Hampshire, started crying because of her sick dog.
- Jessica, a waitress on Long Island, never came back to our table—on two different visits.
- Monica, a waitress in Havre de Grace, Maryland, was visibly shaken because her ex-spouse was marrying her sister the following weekend.
- Todd, a Jew, took a Bible from me and committed to read it.
- Rachel, from Atlanta, asked me to pray for her mom, 46, and step-dad, 26.
- A famous major league home run hitter could not think of anything for me to pray for him.
- Melody, from China, wanted to stay in the states and accepted a Bible from me.
- Amy, a waitress in Flagstaff, broke down and cried at our table.

- Terrance, a waiter in Cincinnati, asked me to pray about reversing his backslidden condition.
- Christine, a waitress in Aberdeen, asked me to pray for her five kids, ages three months to twenty-five years. She wanted to have more children.
- John, an ESPN technician, asked me to pray for him to regain his love for the Word.
- Tai, a fellow passenger on a plane, asked me to pray that he would return to church.
- Lori, a waitress in Old Ripley, Illinois, asked me to pray that she would get back to church.
- Michael, a student at Hope International University, asked me to pray that he would reconnect with God.
- Hannah asked me to pray about a relationship and accepted a Bible from me.
- Rachel, a waitress in Ft. Myers, asked me to pray that she would return to church.
- Jeff, an ER doctor, asked me to pray that he would reconnect with God.
- Shelly, a waitress in Salem, Maryland, asked me to pray that she would return to church.
- Rick, moving to Annapolis, asked me to pray that he would find a church.
- Carrie, a waitress in Kalamazoo, Michigan, asked me to pray for her spiritual growth and for her to find a church.
- Carey, a waitress in Anchorage, Alaska, asked me to pray that she would find a church.
- Amy, a front desk receptionist in Litchfield, Illinois, asked me to pray that she would find a church.
- Pamela, a waitress in Stevensville, Michigan, asked me to pray that she would love Jesus more.

- A former punter with Purdue University and the Cincinnati Bengals asked me to pray for direction.
- A basketball coach at the University of Michigan said that everyone needs prayer.
- A basketball coach at Michigan State University agreed to have me pray for the character of his players.
- A popular comedian asked me to pray for good health.
- Alpacino, a worker at the Salt Lake City airport, named after the famous actor, asked me to pray for his health.
- Dave couldn't tell me what he did for a living, but he wanted me to pray for his daughter.
- Frank, a housing inspector, wanted me to pray for his ability to minister to people.
- Sahar Nusseibeh, former basketball player at American University, asked me to pray for a graduate assistant position somewhere, and she received one at the University of Cincinnati. She is now the assistant basketball coach at Holy Cross.
- Frank, whom I rear-ended in an accident, asked me to pray for alertness for him. (Maybe he was thinking that I should be praying that for myself.)
- Ouida, a lady on the phone from whom I was purchasing a product, asked me to pray for more business. She called me back fifteen minutes later and asked me if I had prayed she had just received a great opportunity for her business.
- Heather, a waitress at Cracker Barrel® gave me her prayer request and then told me that recently two women had also asked her for a prayer request. The two women turned out to be my wife Bonnie and her dear friend Susie.

These were great divine appointments, but they were not in my top 58, which I have written about in the balance of this book.

# CHAPTER 7

# AGAIN?

**I** am settled into my seat; I am readying myself for the short flight from Lansing to Detroit. I am on my way to Council Bluffs, Iowa, to lead a Leadership Retreat for First Christian Church. When I am seated in 4D, I begin talking to my divine appointment in 4C. Her name is Julia, and she is from the town of Haslett, which is right next to my town of Okemos. She is on her way to Maryland to attend the funeral of a friend. Her prayer request is that things will go well; I assure her that I will pray. We part ways in Detroit, and I head to my next flight.

Eight months later, Bonnie and I are headed to Phoenix for a long weekend get-away. I had visited forty-nine states, but I have never been to Arizona. I had a goal to visit all fifty states by the time I was fifty but missed it by a couple of years.

We are in the Detroit airport when our flight to Phoenix is changed. The airline doesn't do well at seating us together on the next flight. I am assigned seat 4D in first class, while Bonnie was in coach. The airline apologizes for the mix-up, but they cannot fix it since first class is full. I offer Bonnie my seat in first class, but she refuses; she just wanted to read a book and relax.

We board our flight together. As we entered the first class cabin, I recognize my divine appointment sitting in 4C. It is Julia again. After I have settled in 4D, I turn to Julia and say, "Your name is Julia, and you are from Haslett."

Startled, she turns to me and asks, "How did you know that?"

Laughing, I reply, "Six months (actually it was eight months) ago you were on your way to Maryland for a funeral. You were in 4C and I was in 4D. I asked you for a prayer request, and you asked me to pray about the funeral."

Now relaxed again, she responds with, "You're a minister, and you live in Okemos, don't you?"

We have a great time chatting on the way to Phoenix; I introduce her to Bonnie in the airport. I am so impressed with God for a variety of reasons. First, He put Julia and me in the exact same seats as before. Second, He helped me to recognize her and remember her name, as well as her prayer request. (I had recorded 131 divine appointments since we had first met eight months earlier.) Third, only our all-powerful God could choose to glorify Himself in situations like this. Who says there is no God?

Divine Appointment Principle #1:
*God loves to surprise us with a clear demonstration of His power. Expect the unexpected.*

# CHAPTER 8

# "ARE WE GOING TO PRAY ABOUT MY REQUEST?"

**M**y dear friend Michael VanDyk and I are in Virginia Beach, Virginia, for some formal coach training. We have both read Tony Stoltzfus's book, *Leadership Coaching,* which God used to really motivate us to take some formal training on coaching.

At the time, Tony still lived in Virginia Beach, so Michael contacts him to see if he will have dinner with us. Tony agrees. We meet at Ruby Tuesday®, and we are having a great time chatting about coaching and life. Our waitress, Laura, takes our order and asks if she can get us anything else.

I explain to her that we always ask for something in our waitress's life that we can pray for over the next month, and I ask her if there is anything in her life that can use prayer.

Laura responds, "I am going back to school next semester, and you could be praying that I do well. I haven't been in school in a couple of years." We commit to pray, and she departs to turn in our orders.

Laura returns to our table a few times, delivering food and getting us more water. Finally she asks me, "Are we going to pray about my request?"

A little surprised, I respond, "How about right now?" So we join hands and pray right then at our table.

She is so grateful and so excited.

Laura becomes a favorite of ours. Michael and I eat at Ruby Tuesday® again on that trip and have Laura for our waitress. Six months later we are back in Virginia Beach for more training, so we request a seat in Laura's section. On our third trip into Virginia Beach, we connect with Laura again. I am so impressed with God that He made this a very special divine appointment. It very well could have been a regular divine appointment if Laura had not asked, "Are we going to pray about my request?" God led us to the right place at the right time. He is so good at that!

Divine Appointment Principle #2:
*I must be ready to instantly respond to where God is leading. Be flexible.*

# CHAPTER 9

# "ARE YOU AN ANGEL?"

**I** am flying out of Lansing to Pittsburgh, and we have just left the gate. I am sitting next to a lady named Renee. I ask her what I can pray for her. She blurts out that she is ready to leave her husband of four years and move back to Philadelphia with her twin two-year-olds.

I am a little amazed at her vulnerability but purpose to try to encourage her. She explains that she hasn't had much to do with God as an adult. She grew up in a church, but that was it. She misses her family back in Philadelphia, and she is really struggling with her husband.

I try to help her focus on her relationship with God. I explain that He wants to have a relationship with her. As we talk all the way to Pittsburgh, I try to keep us on the subject of God. She agrees to meet with me for lunch sometime after she returns from this trip so I can explain to her how to live out this relationship with God.

We are on our descent into Pittsburgh, when she turns to me and asks, "You know that show on TV about angels?"

I respond, "You mean *Touched by an Angel®*?"

"Yes, that's the one," she replies, and with total seriousness, she asks, "Are you an angel?"

I so want the light above my head to come on, but it doesn't. I answer, "Renee, I'm not an angel, but I am a messenger for God. He wants to have a relationship with you."

45

We part ways in the terminal. As I am walking to my next flight, all I can think is, "God, you are so funny!"

I did have the opportunity to later plant some seeds with her, and I am trusting God that He is bringing about spiritual growth in Renee's life. She did leave her husband and move to Philadelphia. I have not seen her for years, but I continue to pray for her.

Divine Appointment Principle #3:
*Our God has a real sense of humor. He shows us that side of Himself so we can laugh with Him.*

# CHAPTER 10

# CHANGE OF PLANS

The agent behind the Delta Airlines® counter is trying to explain why the airline cannot get me to Atlanta that day. I have a scheduled flight from Lansing to Cincinnati, and then to Atlanta, but the Cincinnati to Atlanta flight has been canceled. She assures me that they will get me there by 8 PM. I say that normally 8 PM would be fine, except that today I am leading a seminar beginning at 7 PM. She replies that she is sorry, but she can't get me there any sooner. I look down the row of airline counters in the Lansing airport and ask her if one of them can get me to Atlanta on time. She says that she will try, but she doubts if anyone will take my ticket. She is surprised that Continental Airlines® says "yes," so she sends me down to speak with them.

The agent explains that they will fly me to Cleveland, and then on to Atlanta. I will arrive in plenty of time. So I take the first flight from Lansing to Cleveland, and I go to my gate for the Atlanta flight. Checking in at the gate, I am told that I am on standby since the flight is full. So I sit down and wait and pray. God is up to something. I am mainly interested in arriving in Atlanta on time, but He is working on something else. I am called back to the counter and am given a boarding pass for the flight to Atlanta. I am excited.

On the flight to Atlanta, I sit next to Mike. As we chat, he asks me where I am headed. I tell him that I am leading a weekend seminar at a church in Douglasville. He is totally surprised because that's where he lives. He asks me, "Which church?" I tell him, and he knows exactly where it is. He can't attend the seminar because he is helping someone move this weekend, but he says he would like to check out the church.

God really blesses the weekend seminar at the church. I share with the people at the church about my divine appointment with Mike. I tell them that we have an incredible God. He knew I was headed to Atlanta, and He wanted to connect me with Mike, but Mike was flying out of Cleveland. So God decided to cancel my flight out of Cincinnati and send me to Cleveland instead. That way, He could put me next to Mike on the flight to Atlanta. To you or me, that would be a major undertaking. For God, all He had to do was speak it into existence.

I receive a phone call late the following Wednesday evening from some friends who attend the Douglasville church. They are excited because Mike and his wife, Kim, have attended the Bible study at the church that evening. I am blown away. God is so good.

A few weeks later I receive another phone call from my friends in Douglasville. This time they tell me that Mike and Kim have been baptized tonight. I am speechless. We serve a phenomenal God! I still smile when I think of Mike and how God drastically changed my flight plans to Atlanta. You explain to me why anyone would choose not to serve this all-powerful God.

Divine Appointment Principle #4:
*When God abruptly changes your plans, expect a divine appointment.*

CHAPTER 11

# "DID I JUST HIT YOUR CAR?"

You never know how a divine appointment will take place. I am sitting in my SUV, waiting for Bonnie to come out of a store. It is a pleasant day; I have the windows rolled down. A car pulls into the parking spot next to me. It's bumper hits my driver's side rear tire and jolts my vehicle.

I get out and assess the damage. There is none. The driver gets out of her car and asks, "Did I just hit your car?"

I respond, "Yes, but there is no damage." She introduces herself as Melissa and apologizes for not being more careful. I assure her that it is fine. I figure that this is a divine appointment, so I ask her for a prayer request.

She requests that I pray for a job for her boyfriend, Chad. She goes on to explain that he really needs one. I say that I will pray.

As she enters the store, I think, "God, you are so clever. How many ways can you orchestrate a divine appointment for me when I am just sitting in my parked vehicle?" He is really good!

Divine Appointment #5:
*In the midst of a temptation to respond emotionally, look for God's bigger picture.*

CHAPTER 12

# "DO YOU BELIEVE IN PRAYER?"

**I** don't know about you, but I dislike having to mail anything at the post office. I don't dislike the people; I dislike the customer service that I typically experience. I have often thought that you could meet someone in line at the post office and be engaged to them before you reach the counter.

On one particular day, I have to mail out some of my teaching CDs. Sure enough, when I arrive, the line is outside the lobby. I grudgingly take my place in line. I am directly behind an Asian lady, and I am thinking about how I can begin a conversation with her. It is always easier to start a conversation with someone behind you. You simply turn around, make eye contact, and begin speaking. It is much more difficult to have a conversation with someone facing the opposite direction.

I am significantly taller than the Asian lady, and she is preoccupied, reading a letter. The letter is from the government, and it explains why she is at the post office. I am so bored that I am reading the letter over the lady's shoulder. All at once, my cell phone rings. I normally set it to vibrate when I enter a building, but I had forgotten to do so. The call is from one of my accountability partners, and he is rejoicing at an incredible answer to prayer. I am making comments such as, "God really answers prayer" and "Wow, God is good." I finally finish the call and set my cell phone to vibrate.

Suddenly the Asian lady turns around and questions me, "Do you believe in prayer?"

I respond that I do, and we have a great chat for a couple of minutes on prayer and following Jesus. Then before I can ask her about praying for something in her life, she is at the counter.

As God can orchestrate life, we both finish our business at the counter at the same time and walk out of the post office together. I ask her for a prayer request, and she replies, "Dean, just pray for patience for me."

Now I have to decide if I should go into a short "sermonette" explaining to her that you don't ask God for patience or if I should just let it go. I decide to let it go and commit to pray for her.

As we part company, I am so impressed with God that He can even give me a divine appointment in line at the post office when I am bored. He really is good!

Divine Appointment #6:
*God has the ability to make things exciting even when I am bored.*

# CHAPTER 13

# "DO YOU READ ENGLISH?"

I am getting ready to co-lead a seminar in Chiang Mai, Thailand. I am excited. I have never been to Thailand before. There are seventeen of us making the trip to Thailand and then to Kunming, China. Our team leader is instructing us about all the things we will be doing and what we will need to bring. I am planning to bring a few Mandarin Bibles with me to give away. I really don't know why, but I pack a couple of English Bibles anyway.

Everyone else is from Alaska, so I fly there to join up with the team. I arrive late in the day, and we fly out of Anchorage on my birthday at 2 AM. We have a little birthday celebration at the airport before we leave. (We cross the International Date Line within a few hours, so it will be my shortest birthday ever.)

We are scheduled to fly to Taipei, then to Bangkok, and finally to Chiang Mai. On the flight from Taipei to Bangkok, I sit next to an Asian man who is my divine appointment. His English is broken, but we communicate well. I discover that he was originally from Myanmar but now lives in San Francisco. He explains that he has received his visa to move to the States, but his wife is still waiting for hers. They expect her wait to be about five more years, so each year he will travel back to Myanmar to visit her for a short period.

I tell him that I am impressed with his English. I then ask him, "Do you read English?"

He exclaims, "I read everything I can get my hands on. It is good practice for me."

I tell him that I have a gift for him and present him with one of my two English Bibles. He is so delighted to receive it. He explains, "One of my friends back in San Francisco told me last week that if I wanted to really learn English, I should read a Christian Bible." Within one week, God arranged for someone to give him one! Wow! Our God is amazing.

I still have one English Bible left. After the seminar, we travel to Kunming and spend a few days praying and encouraging people. On the flight out of Kunming to Hong Kong, I sit next to a Japanese father and his daughter. After we have talked for a while, I ask him if he and his daughter would like an English Bible, and he says "Yes." I give them my other English Bible.

We spend about twenty-four hours in Hong Kong debriefing the significance of our time together. It is a great place. We fly out of Hong Kong to Taipei, and then board a flight to Anchorage. I expect the flight to have several empty seats, but it is full. I am seated next to a couple from Beijing. She is a doctor and speaks some English, but her husband does not. As we cross the International Date Line, I hand her a Mandarin Bible, explaining, "This is your 'welcome to America' gift." I don't think that she had ever seen a Bible before. She reads it for two hours, and then gives it to her husband, who reads it for another two hours. Is our God great or what?

On this trip, I am able to bless people from Myanmar, Japan, and China with Bibles of their own.

Our God is very impressive and very intentional with sharing His Word, even with strangers in a divine appointment! He is unstoppable and relentless in making His truth known.

Divine Appointment #7:
*God is even more interested than we are in having people read His Word.*

CHAPTER 14

# "DO YOU TEACH ON PRAYER?"

I am on my way home from the same trip to Asia that you read about in the previous chapter. I was with the group from Anchorage, Alaska, who has organized the trip. It has been a great two weeks, but I am ready to be home for a while. On this trip I have had the opportunity to teach in Thailand and in China; God has stretched me in a variety of ways. We reach Anchorage before noon. I sleep a little, shower, and head back to the airport for my "red eye" flight to Minneapolis. I am really hoping to sleep on the four-hour plus flight.

I am sitting in an aisle seat with no one next to me. I think that this is ideal since I want to sleep anyway. The lady two seats over and next to the window starts complaining to the flight attendant that she wants an aisle seat. The flight attendant explains that there are no aisle seats available. I am beginning to mull over in my mind if I should just change seats with her and get to the bliss of sleeping.

At that moment, a couple behind me speak up and offer their aisle seat to the lady. Before I know it, this sweet couple is sitting next to me. We talk for a while as the crew is getting the plane ready to leave the gate. Clay and Kristin ask me what brought me to Anchorage. I describe to them the trip I have just completed and how I had connected with Faith Community Christian Church when I was in Anchorage a few months ago.

They ask, "Do you teach on prayer?"

Not sure why they would ask such a question, I reply in the affirmative.

Clay explains, "My mother attends that church, and she sure enjoyed your seminar. She was so excited and couldn't say enough good things about the weekend."

Then he adds, "Kristin and I have a hundred questions about prayer, and we can't believe that we are sitting next to you on this long flight." Oh, well, so much for sleep! Instead, we discuss prayer all the way to Minneapolis. It is great conversation; I thoroughly enjoy my time with them. In the Minneapolis airport, we spend more time together, and we have someone take our picture. It is a marvelous divine appointment. God is so creative at putting the right people in my path at just the right time—even when I have plans to enjoy a relaxing nap.

Divine Appointment Principle #8:
*Sometimes I want to rest, but God wants me to bless others through a divine appointment. I can trust Him to know and take care of my needs.*

CHAPTER 15

# "DON'T EXPECT THAT EVERY TIME."

I am teaching a Saturday seminar at the Manchester Christian Church in Manchester, New Hampshire. One of the workshops that I am leading is on divine appointments. A gentleman approaches me after that session and tells me how delighted he is to learn about divine appointments. He desires to put into practice what he has just learned. I encourage him to do so.

I receive a note by e-mail from him later that day. He explains that he ate lunch in a local restaurant. He asked his waitress for a prayer request, and they both ended up on the floor on their knees, praying for her request. How wild is that!

I send him an e-mail back, "That's great! Don't expect that every time."

I am amazed at how God can move supernaturally in big ways when we are attempting to be obedient to Him in small ways. He is an incredible God!

Divine Appointment Principle #9:
*Some divine appointments are routine. Others are amazingly wild. Go with what God orchestrates.*

# CHAPTER 16

# GETTING HOME EARLIER

I am flying out of Tampa back to Michigan one January day. My flight is scheduled for 2 PM, but I am trying hard to catch an earlier flight. My scheduled flight will not allow me to reach home until midnight. I call Delta Airlines® to see if I can take an earlier flight, but they assure me that there are no open seats before my flight. My flight is to take me to Memphis, then Detroit, and finally Lansing. It is going to be a long afternoon and evening!

I go to the airport early, just in case. At check in, the agent assures me once again that there is no way I can fly out earlier than my scheduled flight at 2 PM. I give up on my plan, I go through security and on to my gate. I am three hours early. I had prayed all day that God would help me to arrive home earlier than midnight.

My flight is to leave from Gate 7 at 2 PM. As I sit reading in the terminal near Gate 7, I notice that another flight is leaving shortly after mine from Gate 9. It is going straight to Detroit, and it will have me there much sooner than the two flights through Memphis. But then I remember that the Delta® agent has told me that she cannot get me home sooner on any other flight.

As we are nearing the time to board my flight, the gate agent makes an announcement that the flight is overbooked; they are going to give passengers a $300 travel voucher for taking a different flight. I am at the counter in a matter of seconds. The agent checks out the possibilities of putting me on a different flight. She makes me smile when she says that a seat has opened up on the direct flight to Detroit and asks if I would mind arriving home six hours early. I am tempted to say that I would pay Delta® $300 for that to happen, but I decide to keep my mouth shut and just accept their offer. She issues my boarding pass and my travel voucher; I happily move over to Gate 9.

I am praising God for the opportunity to arrive home earlier with a $300 travel voucher in my possession. I am even upgraded to first class for the flight to Detroit. As we are boarding the flight, the same agent from Gate 7 is now scanning the boarding passes at Gate 9. When I hand her my boarding pass, she says, "Merry Christmas!" Since it is January, my confusion is evident to her. She explains that she doesn't need my seat after all, but the airline has left me on the flight to Detroit anyway, and I am allowed to keep my voucher. I am ecstatic, to say the least! I am so impressed with God that I am giddy.

I sit down in my assigned seat of 2A next to a fellow traveler in 2B. I am wildly explaining to him how God miraculously put me on this flight with a $300 travel voucher to boot. As I eventually ask him for a prayer request, he explains to me that this is his first flight in quite a while. The last time he flew, he had a problem with his heart and ended up in a hospital in Phoenix. He is a little nervous. He desperately wants a trip without any health issues. He asks if I would be willing to pray for his family also. Then it hits me. This is not about me or even my getting home six hours early with a $300 travel voucher. It is all about me sitting next to him so that I can pray for him and encourage him. We have a great conversation during the flight to Michigan that encourages both of us.

Here are some lessons from that day.

1. When I pray selfishly, He still has the ability to answer that prayer according to His higher purposes. His grace overwhelms me!

2. When I am praying for something physical (to arrive home early), God has a way of refocusing my attention on the spiritual. We serve an awesome God!

I am speechless at God's generosity!

Divine Appointment Principle #10:
*God will work far beyond my own self-serving desires.*

CHAPTER 17

# "GIRLFRIEND?"

I am leading a seminar at Northeast Christian Church in Grand Junction, Colorado. A few of us, including my friend Michael Chase, the pastor, decide to meet together for dinner at one of the local restaurants. They ask me to decide which restaurant, and when given the choice, I often select a Texas Roadhouse® or a similar restaurant because it usually has sweet potatoes on the menu. I love them.

Before leaving for the restaurant, I ask God what we should be praying for our waiter or waitress that evening. What I sense is a prompting to pray about a girlfriend situation.

Our waiter that evening is Sean. We have a great time joking around with him. I finally ask him what we can pray for him over the next month. He explains that he is a graduating senior, and he would like to find a great job after college. That is a fairly common prayer request from college students.

When he leaves our table, God reminds me that I need to pray about Sean's girlfriend's situation. When Sean returns, I ask him if he has a girlfriend; he says that he does. He explains that she is a freshman at his university and that she had been living with her parents until they moved out of state. She doesn't really have a place to stay, so she has moved in with him. Now it is clear to me why God wanted me to pray for the girlfriend situation. Sean could have just affirmed that he had a girlfriend and said nothing more. But our God moved him to share enough information so that we knew exactly what to be praying for Sean and his girlfriend. I prayed for a long while that Sean and his girlfriend would find Jesus together and choose to live in obedience to God's truth. I am often surprised at how specifically God wants us to pray for people that He brings across our paths. It requires listening. I personally need to become a better listener.

Divine Appointment Principle #11:
*People don't need our judgment; they need our prayers.*

CHAPTER **18**

# "GO SEE THE PRESIDENT"

**I** am leading a Prayer Journey in the city of Portland, Oregon. It is a beautiful city in a beautiful state. I love the Northwest. We pray in various places around the city. We locate some great high elevations from which we can pray as we look over the city.

One day we decide to go west of the city to Forest Grove to pray on the campus of Pacific University. We arrive on campus and park. There are about eight of us on the prayer team this morning. I give instructions and send people off in different directions. We have purposed to meet back at our original location in about 90 minutes.

I head off to the north side of campus and spend some time just praying and listening. About thirty minutes into this time with God, I sense the prompting, "Go see the President."

I am pretty sure that this is from God because I was not even thinking about the president. I have no idea who is the president of this university, and I certainly have no idea where his office is located.

I notice a building not far from where I am sitting, so I head over to check it out. Just inside the door, I notice a directory on the wall; the president's office is on the third floor. I go up to the third floor and ask his secretary if he is in his office. She states that he is, but someone is with him in a meeting. She asks me to wait, and she will let him know I am here to see him when the meeting is over. I go out in the hallway and sit down. I am really hoping that this is of God.

Within a few minutes, she invites me into the president's office and introduces me. I am impressed with his graciousness; he asks what he can do for me. I explain that a small group of us is on the campus this morning praying, and I would like to know what we should be praying for him and for the university.

He asks me to pray for guidance; then he explains why. I thank him and then leave. I am so excited that God put me on the president's docket that morning. I want to live each day believing that He can put me on anyone's docket because He is that good.

Divine Appointment Principle #12:
*I need to simply obey, regardless of whether it makes sense to me at the moment.*

# CHAPTER 19

# "GOD, HELP ME FIND HER"

In my campus ministry days at Michigan State University, I enjoyed the opportunities to connect with students and encourage them to grow spiritually. A church in the Detroit area, which supported our campus ministry, sent me the name of a young lady from the church who was new to MSU. They asked me to visit her and to invite her to a fellowship meeting. I committed to do so.

After I met her in her residence hall, she visited one of our weekly meetings. I thought things went well, and she seemed to enjoy herself.

A few days later I received word from her minister. He said that she thought we were some weird organization, and she had totally misinterpreted something that was said in the meeting. He thanked me for inviting her to our meeting and asked me if I could clear things up with her. I appreciated his confidence in our ministry, and I felt compelled to speak with this young lady right away. I called her room, but she was not there, and her roommate didn't know where she was or when she would return.

Because I so wanted to speak with her right away, I went out on campus looking for her and praying, "God, help me find her." Now understand that the main part of campus is four square miles, and on any given day there are 42,000 students and 10,000 faculty and staff around campus. I had to meet someone else over on the west side of campus, so I headed over there first.

As I was driving by the old intramural building, I saw her walking in front of it. I parked my car and caught up with her. We had a good conversation and cleared up her misunderstanding.

As I returned to my car and headed off to my next meeting, I thought about God's greatness. To simply say that He is awesome is a vast understatement. He is able to do exceedingly, abundantly beyond what I can think or imagine. He had just shown me that one more time.

Divine Appointment Principle #13:
*God can lead me to anyone at anytime because He knows exactly where he or she is at the moment.*

# CHAPTER 20

# GOD KNOWS WHAT I NEED TO LEARN TODAY

I have received an invitation to fill in for a preacher whose father had passed away during the week. I am looking forward to the opportunity. I have not preached at this church before, but I have co-led a coaching seminar there.

As I am preparing for Sunday, God encourages me to take a different twist on a topic that I have taught before. I am wondering what He has in mind for me and whom He desires for me to specifically encourage.

Upon my arrival this morning, I discover that the church has invited someone to come in that morning to lead worship. The congregation has had a major service project on Saturday for their city, and some of the staff, including the regular worship leader, were given this Sunday morning off. The church has both a guest speaker and a guest worship leader today.

The guest worship leader, Andy Schroeder, and I have met before. I enjoy catching up on what God is doing in his life. He explains to me that he had left a worship leading position with a church several months ago, and he has begun working with a service ministry. He really sensed it was God leading him to make the change. Now because of finances, he is being forced to leave the service ministry, and he is not sure what to do next. He is blaming himself for making the move to the service ministry and believes that he should never have left the worship leading position.

I reassure Andy that it could have been God who led him to make the change, even though He knew it was going to be a short-term position. God can lead us through such transitions

71

to teach us how to trust Him. I relate to Andy how God had led Bonnie and me to purchase a house down the street with the idea of selling our current house. Our house did not sell for three and a half years. We experienced financial pressure greater than ever. During that time, Satan was trying to convince us that we were really stupid for buying the new house and that we hadn't heard God accurately.

Bonnie and I backtracked the process of hearing from God and purchasing the new house. We concluded that He actually led us into that decision. God built volumes of trust in us for Him in the three and a half years. We hadn't made a mistake; God was growing our faith in Him. (Over the course of the three and a half years, I had often prayed, "God, just send an angel to buy the house. I really don't care if the buyers are human." As I was reading the purchase agreement that finally came, I noticed the names of the buyers: John and Deborah Angell. God is so funny!)

As I share our story with Andy, it seems to resonate with him. God then turns on the "light bulb." The primary reason that God has me here today is not mainly to bless someone from this church, but to really bless and encourage Andy. He is my divine appointment. Wow! Our God is so good at orchestrating people into our lives so we can learn from them or for them to learn from us. He knows exactly what we need to learn today.

Divine Appointment Principle #14:
*My perceived purpose for being in a place may be totally different from God's actual purpose.*

CHAPTER **21**

# "GOD, CLOSE THIS PLACE DOWN"

**I** am curious to see what God is going to do. My home church is having an Easter service at an area high school with the idea of inviting the community to attend. People from the church have been encouraged to invite their friends and neighbors. The staff has printed some fliers to distribute to family and friends. I am in town the week before Easter, so I contact the church office to see what I can do to help. Barb explains that we still need to place some fliers in the businesses around the high school. I pick up the fliers and drive to the area near the high school.

I don't know how businesses will respond to my request, but I expect that the worst that can happen is for the owner to say "No!" I find that many of the businesses are happy to know about the Easter service and are very willing to post our flier. About 10 AM, I find myself in the parking lot of a strip club. It is advertised as "Lansing's only all nude nightclub." I am thinking, "Hey, I wonder if they will post a flier for us."

The parking lot is empty, but I decide to try the door anyway; it is locked. I figure that these people are nocturnal, so I return to my car. I make a deal with God. If I have one flier left after circling this four-block area, I will return and ask them to post a flier. Sure enough, after completing the four-block circle, I have one flier left. It is about 11:30 AM, and there are now cars in the parking lot. I grab my flier and enter the front door into the lobby. A gentleman sitting on a couch asks me what he can do for me, explaining that he is the manager. I show him the flier and ask if he will post it for us. He replies enthusiastically, "Sure, we can do that!" I think that we are on a roll here, so I ask him for his first name. He tells me, and as I am heading toward the door, I ask him what I can be praying for him. He laughs and says, "You can pray for anything you want." I tell him, "Thanks," and then I leave. Out in the parking lot, I start praying that God will close this place down. After all, I have the manager's permission!

Over time I have prayed a wide variety of prayers concerning that business. Whenever I pass that place, I have prayed whatever God puts on my heart. I have prayed for Him to make the place invisible so that people could not find it. I have prayed for financial problems, employees to be temporarily sick and miss work, employees to quit their jobs, and about anything else you can imagine.

The place is still in business, but I really believe that God has done some good things, and He has not written the last chapter yet on the strip club. I once met a former employee who is now a Christian. Some might think that places like this should be picketed. I am not opposed to that, but I think God's greatest power is demonstrated when His people pray. I continue to pray for God to close down the strip club. He is more than able.

Divine Appointment Principle #15:
*Don't say "No" for other people. Ask the question anyway.*
*God may open an amazing, unexpected door.*

# CHAPTER 22

# "GOD, WHERE DID SHE GO?"

**I** am traveling to St. Joseph, Michigan, to lead a seminar this Saturday morning. I am driving westbound across I-94, and I am running a little late. I am still a half hour away from the church building. As I approach exit 41, I look across the expressway and spot a car off the side of the road; a woman is standing next to it. The car's hood is up. God prompts me to stop and see if I can help. I think about it for a second, wondering if this extra delay will make me late for the seminar. Now I sense a stronger need to stop; however, I am already past the exit ramp.

Fortunately, there is another exit at mile marker 39, so I pull off that exit and enter I-94 going the opposite direction. I pull up behind the car and get out; the woman is nowhere in sight. I notice that apparently the engine in her car has dropped to the ground.

I am thinking, "God, where did she go? I know you wanted me to stop." I return to my car and look for a turn-around so I can head west again. At exit 41, I see a woman walking down the exit ramp. I pull onto the ramp and stop my car beside her to ask if I can help in any way. She says that she needs a wrecker and that she is heading to a service station at this exit. I offer her a ride; she introduces herself as Sharon and says that she is grateful for the ride. We pull into a service station, and I tell her that I will be praying for her. She says, "OK, thanks," and bows her head. I wasn't thinking about praying right that minute, but if she is willing, why not? I pray for her and ask God to bless her immensely. She murmurs, "Thank you" and quickly runs into the gas station.

I get back on westbound I-94 and drive toward the church. I arrived in time for the seminar, and God certainly blesses it. I conclude that God sometimes prompts us with commands just to see if we will obey. I think that this is one such instance in my life.

Divine Appointment Principle #16:
*God can interrupt our schedule at any time He chooses, and He may be testing our willingness to obey His prompting.*

CHAPTER 23

# "GOD, YOU WENT TO A GREAT DEAL OF TROUBLE"

**I** am flying this morning to Orlando, Florida, to lead a seminar in Melbourne. It is January, and the thought of spending the weekend in warm, sunny Florida as opposed to Michigan sounds like a gracious gift from the Lord.

I have flown into Detroit Metro from Lansing, and I am seated in 3B for the noon flight to Orlando. I am waiting for the boarding to be completed so we can take off for the Sunshine State. I have been upgraded to first class; it is full except for the seat next to me. The door is about to close, when suddenly an Asian lady dashes aboard the plane and slips into the vacant seat. She introduces herself as Kim.

She works for the airline and is headed to Orlando. She and her husband left San Francisco yesterday, flying the employee plan. They flew into Detroit and planned on catching an evening flight to Orlando. There was only one open seat on that flight, so they decided to spend the night in Detroit and catch the 7 AM flight to Orlando. There was only one open seat on that flight as well, so she sent her husband to Orlando and waited for the 10 AM flight. There were no open seats on that flight either; she tried this noon flight. There was only one open seat, and it was next to me.

I am thinking, "God, you went to a great deal of trouble to get this woman to sit next to me."

She finds out that I am a Christian and that I am heading to Melbourne to lead a seminar this weekend. She identifies herself as a Christian. She states that she was baptized a few years ago, but she doesn't attend any church.

I finally get around to asking her for a prayer request, and she immediately asks me to pray for her daughter, who is a senior at UCLA. Kim is concerned that her daughter is becoming an atheist; she wants me to pray that her daughter will not. I must have taken some "bold" pills that morning by mistake because I respond to Nina's request by answering, "Maybe your daughter is becoming an atheist because she doesn't see Jesus in your life."

Kim asks, "What do you mean?"

I explain that if Kim never lives out her faith and never attends church, how is her daughter ever going to see the impact of Jesus on Kim's life? I go on to suggest that maybe God put her next to me on this flight so that she will repent of her casual relationship with God and purpose to live fully devoted to Him.

She questions, "What would that look like?"

I suggest that she pray to God asking Him to forgive her of her non-existent relationship with Him and telling Him that she wants to serve Him now and in the future.

She replies, "Dean, I have never prayed out loud."

I continue, "I believe that God is giving you this window of opportunity to make your life right with Him."

Right then our food trays are set down in front of us, so I take her hand and say that I will pray for our food.

After lunch, I am thinking that we are getting closer and closer to Orlando, and Kim's window of opportunity is closing. We are about thirty minutes out of Orlando, when Kim speaks up and says, "Dean, I am ready to pray."

I know that this is going to be a profoundly moving prayer time. I take her hand and assure her that I will be praying for her while she is praying to God. She says, "OK," and begins her quiet prayer.

"Oh God, it has been a long time since I have talked to you." She then goes off on a tangent that doesn't have anything to do with what she needs to be praying.

So I am silently praying, "God, that is a tangent. Bring her back, please."

All of a sudden, she says, "Oh God, that is a tangent. This is what I need to say." She prays a heartfelt prayer of repentance. She has tears running down her face, and so do I.

She sighs, "That was good."

I agree. I ask her if she has a Bible; she says "No." I promise to send her one, and she gives me her home address.

At the Orlando airport, Kim introduces me to her husband. We have a great time chatting about the events of the day. As we depart in different directions, I wondered what Kim's life will be like now. She has encountered God at 30,000 feet; I pray that she will live devoted to Him on the ground. Our God is amazing!

Divine Appointment Principle #17:
*God often expects us to show boldness, but He always expects us to show love.*

# CHAPTER 24

# GOD'S PERFECT SPLIT-SECOND TIMING

I am flying home from Baltimore one Monday morning after leading a weekend seminar at Fork Christian Church in Fork, Maryland. I prayed this morning that God would give me a special divine appointment on my way home. Unbeknownst to me, Bonnie has also prayed for a special divine appointment during my trip home.

On my first flight into Detroit, I sit next to a couple from Frankenmuth, Michigan; we have a great time chatting. I ask for a prayer request and receive one. They also ask me what they can be praying for me. It is a good divine appointment, but it is not really "special."

It seems that God often provides divine appointments in the midst of a change or an interruption. I go to my gate in the Detroit airport and wait for my flight to Lansing. While I am sitting in the gate area, the gate agent announces that there is a problem with our aircraft, so we will be taking a different plane to Lansing from a different gate. Along with the other passengers, I walk to my new gate and wait again. I sit down in an area next to some luggage, but no one else is sitting there. Within a short while, two flight attendants sit down next to me. They are working the Lansing flight. I discover that Cindy, the lead flight attendant, lives in a city that I have visited on several occasions. Before I can ask her for a prayer request, the gate agent calls the flight crew on board to prepare the plane for our departure.

As I board the plane for Lansing, Cindy is at the door greeting passengers. I stop and quickly tell her, "Cindy, I always look for something in people's lives that I can pray for them. Please give some thought to that and let me know before I deplane what I can pray for you." She says that she will. I sit next to two ladies from Arkansas, and we have a great time talking about their trip to Michigan. They give me a prayer request; I assure them that I will be praying. Once again, it is a good divine appointment, but it is not anything "special."

About halfway into the flight, another flight attendant comes to my seat, introduces herself as Alysia, and asks if she can speak with me. I have no idea what she is going to say, and I think that maybe I have done something wrong. She tells me that she heard me ask Cindy for a prayer request; she wants to know if I will pray for her. I assure her that I will absolutely do so, and she shares her request. Alysia goes back to work, and I think, "Now *that* was special."

As I am deplaning, I walk by Alysia, and she says, "Please don't forget about me." I give her a hug and reiterate that I will be praying. Cindy is at the door again. As I approach her, she hands me a note and says, "I wish we had time to talk right now, but I need to take this plane right back to Detroit." I commit to pray for her and leave the plane. In the terminal, I open the note and read it. It says, "Please pray for my husband Jim and I that we would have peace, love, and trust in our marriage. Blessings to you." I am amazed at God's ability to bring people across my path that have specific prayer needs. Two flight attendants on the same flight, and they both have heavy hearts. God is so good! I don't see Cindy or Alysia over the next year.

I keep expecting to see them on one of my flights, but it does not happen. In the ensuing months, I introduce myself to a lady who works at the entrance of the flight crew lounge. I stop and talk with her when I am in that part of the airport. She has asked me to be praying about her daughter, so I check in with her from time to time for an update. I tell her about Cindy and Alysia, but she does not know them personally. I ask her to be looking for them because I want an update.

I am flying through Detroit one day; I have not been in the Detroit airport for about a month. My flight into Detroit is late. I have a long way to go for my next flight, but I want to check with the lady at the entrance of the flight crew lounge to see if she has met Cindy or Alysia. I am about five feet from the door when a flight attendant steps out of the lounge. I glance at the nametag. It is Alysia! It has been over a year. She is walking away from me down the concourse. I call, "Alysia!" She turns, looks at me and asks, "Who are you?" I say, "You are Alysia _____" (I said her last name). She looks at me and says, "You have been praying for me, haven't you?" I answer, "Yes" and give her a hug. We have a quick chat, and she brings me up-to-date concerning her prayer request. I am so impressed with God's timing. I was late; if Alysia had walked out of the lounge one second earlier or one second later, I would have missed her.

I often run into Alysia. She has met Bonnie, and we have thoroughly enjoyed our "chance" meetings on planes or in the Detroit airport. Some time later, I am flying out of Flint into Detroit, and I have been upgraded to first class. I am in 3C, getting to know the gentleman in 3D. The flight crew begins to give their normal preflight instructions. I notice that Alysia is the flight attendant giving the instructions for first class. She doesn't see me at first, but then we make eye contact, and she is all smiles. When she finishes with the instructions, she stops by my seat and gives me a big hug. We talk for a few seconds; she goes back to work. My new friend in 3D says, "Wow, you must fly a lot!"

Divine Appointment Principle #18:
*God's orchestrating is split-second perfect.*

# CHAPTER 25

# HILKA

Statistics tell us that Christians make up about 1% of the population of the Czech Republic. Nothing I have observed during my several trips there would lead me to challenge those numbers. Still Prague is one of my favorite cities to visit in Europe. I love Old Town Square. There you will see the statue of Jan Hus, who was martyred for his Christian faith. You will also see twenty-seven crosses in the pavement representing two guillotines and twenty-five noblemen who were beheaded because of their part in the Reformation.

On this particular day, some of us from Impact Ministries International, a campus ministry organization, are praying around the city. We decide to eat together at KFC® near the center of the city. The restaurant is crowded, and we are scattered across four lines waiting to place our orders. As I reach the head of the line, a young lady attempts to take my order in Czech. When I reply in English, she responds in English as well. Her name is Hilka. While I am waiting for my order, she asks me why I am in Prague. I explain that our Christian ministry is having a meeting here, and we have also been praying for the city. She surprises me with, "I am Christian also." I ask her which church she attends; she regretfully responds, "I have not found one yet."

Now I am really excited. I tell her that I want her to meet someone. I grab my food and look around the restaurant for Marek, who is our Impact team leader in Prague. I introduce Marek to Hilka, and they purpose to get together soon.

I am so impressed with God. You could wander around the city of Prague for months and never find a Christian looking for a church. So much of what God does in our lives is simply supernatural. We just need to show up.

Divine Appointment Principle #19:
*Finding a needle in a haystack is an everyday occurrence for God.*

# CHAPTER 26

# HOKKAIDO UNIVERSITY

**I** am leading a prayer journey on the campus of Hokkaido University in Sapporo, Japan. Approximately one half of one percent of the Japanese people claim to be a Christian of any kind. It is certainly not common to meet a Christian anywhere in Japan, let alone on a university campus.

We want to be praying and listening to what God wants to communicate to us. It is a beautiful campus, and the eight of us are enjoying our time there.

God really surprises us in His ability to orchestrate divine appointments. He is amazing. We have a total of three divine appointments on campus. Each person approaching us initiates the divine appointment, and all three encounters are with Christians. Only God can do that! It is one more reminder that our God is always at work, regardless of whether we can see it or not. We serve a powerful God!

Divine Appointments Principle #20:
*God can affirm what I am doing through a divine appointment even when I am not looking for it.*

CHAPTER **27**

# "HOW MUCH MONEY DO YOU NEED?"

Five of us pile into a car and begin a search to find a place to eat. We are attending a conference in Aurora, Colorado, and this night we are on our own for dinner. We pass some restaurants and finally settle on a T.G.I. Friday's®.

The hostess directs us to our table, and we sit down. Peter, our waiter, takes our drink orders and delivers them. After he has taken our food order, I ask Peter what we can pray for him. He immediately replies that we can pray for his brother Adam, who needs to get some things straightened out in his life.

While we are enjoying our food and conversation, Peter comes back to the table with another prayer request. He explains that one of the other waiters at the restaurant, Ricky, is trying to get back home to another state to see his dad, who is in a hospital and not doing well. The employees at the restaurant are collecting money for a plane ticket for Ricky. We ask, "How much money do you need?" After consulting the manager, he returns with the information that they are short about $40. We tell him that we will be praying for Ricky.

We decide that we can gather the $40 ourselves. We pool our money and call Peter back to our table. We give him the $40, and he is overwhelmed, to say the least. Within a few minutes, the manager arrives to express his gratitude. He wants to know who we are and why we are giving the money. We tell him we heard there was a need, and we want to help. He can't believe it. A waitress hears about our gift, and she stops at our table, wanting to speak with us. We receive a prayer request from her also.

We leave the restaurant that evening blessed that God has allowed us to bless someone else. What an awesome divine appointment! God reminds me afterward that when His people are generous and love others, the world will want to know why. God graciously gave us an opportunity to model His grace. I love it when He does that.

Divine Appointment Principle #21:
*When God's people show up with generosity and with love, the world will want to know why.*

# CHAPTER 28

# "I AM HAVING PROBLEMS WITH MY BOYFRIEND'S EX!"

**B**onnie and I are enjoying the National Missionary Convention. Our dear friends, Mike and Marilyn VanDyk, are helping out at our exhibit booth for Intentional Impact. I am leading three workshops this afternoon; I am excited about sharing some new material.

It is about 11 AM, when I suddenly realize that I do not have my notes with me at the convention center. They are on my laptop back at the hotel, which is twenty miles away. I wouldn't call it a major panic, but it certainly is a minor one.

Bonnie and I rush to our car and drive back to the hotel. I dump my notes on a thumb drive and hurry to the hotel lobby to print them on the guest services computer printer. A hand-written sign on the printer explains that the printer is out of ink. There are some hotel employees sitting in the lobby area, so I ask them about my options.

One of them, Alycia, says, "My office is very cluttered and messy, but if you don't mind that, we can print your file on my printer."

After I assure her that I am not concerned about the condition of her office, she leads me to her office just off the lobby. As we are waiting for my file to print, I ask her if there is something in her life that I can be praying for her over the next month.

With no hesitation, she blurts out, "I'm having problems with my boyfriend's ex. Could you pray about that? I was just telling my co-workers in the lobby how frustrated I am. I don't know what to do next." She sincerely thanks me for asking.

On the way back to the convention center, I tell Bonnie what God did and how amazed I am that God can use us, even in panic mode, to be a blessing to someone who has a need. He is always at work, no matter what mode I am in. He is simply terrific.

Divine Appointment Principle #22:
*In my panic, God doesn't.*

# CHAPTER 29

# "I AM LOOKING FOR A CHRISTIAN CAMPUS GROUP"

I am visiting our campus ministry at the State University of New York at Albany. We planted the campus ministry almost two years ago, and God is definitely blessing it with some quality students. Our staff is doing a great job of growing themselves and helping students to grow. It is a Friday evening, and it is Valentine's Day. (Before you start thinking about why I'm not back in Michigan with Bonnie on Valentine's Day, let me explain that she is on a Caribbean cruise with her dental office, while I'm in the snow in Albany.)

I am heading back to Greg's house where I am spending the evening. He is a very gracious host to allow me to stay with him whenever I am in the area. I am hungry, so I start looking for a place to eat while I am driving north out of Albany. I spot a Ponderosa® and decide I will give it a try. I want something quick (buffet) because I need to get to Greg's and go to bed. I will have a ten-hour drive home tomorrow. The hostess seats me in a somewhat isolated place in the restaurant and tells me that Josh will be my waiter.

Josh arrives at my table, and I like him right away. We discuss several things as I eat my dinner. I ask him what I can pray for him, and he answers, "I am looking for a Christian group on campus at SUNY Albany." I tell him that I work with a Christian campus ministry on that campus; he is so excited to hear about our group. I write down the contact information for our staff on my business card and give it to him. He says that he will attend (and he did).

Driving on to Greg's after dinner, I am overwhelmed with God. Here I am self-centeredly looking for a quick place to eat so I can get a good night's sleep, and God wants to connect me with someone looking for Christian fellowship. I could have eaten in a hundred different places, and I could even have been seated in someone else's section at Ponderosa® instead of Josh's, but God orchestrated a divine appointment of great significance. Wow! I run out of adjectives in attempting to describe our all-powerful God. I think He loves it when I am speechless.

Divine Appointment Principle #23:
*Some divine appointments are searching for something that we have, if only we will take the time to share it.*

# CHAPTER 30

# I AM THE ONLY ONE IN FIRST CLASS

**I** am flying this morning to Texas; I am excited about speaking at a Christian university this week. Mark, the campus minister, has been trying to get me on campus for a while, but the president of the university would not allow him to bring in someone who is not a part of their "brotherhood."

Mark had contacted me almost a year ago and said that he thought things might be coming together for me to speak on campus. I asked him, "What has changed?" He explained that he had just received approval to bring in a woman speaker this year for spiritual renewal week. He believed that if he can get a woman speaker approved, he can probably get me approved for next year. It turned out that he was correct.

I have four flights scheduled for this morning; I have just boarded my third one. I have been upgraded to first class. Much to my surprise, I am the only person in first class. In all my years of flying, this has never happened before. Twice I had been on a smaller plane where there was just one other passenger, and I had received a prayer request both times. (On one of those flights, I personally knew the other passenger.)

The time comes for the flight crew to give us the regular instructions for the flight. The lead flight attendant, Rachel, is ready to instruct me in first class, but it appears that going through the instructions might be a little awkward with just one person. I suggest that she sit down next to me and that

95

maybe I could give her the needed instructions since I have heard them so many times. Rachel does her own instructions, and then we converse about life for a while.

I ask for a prayer request; she immediately has one. She wants to be transferred to the Memphis hub from the Detroit hub since her husband has a job offer in Memphis. I commit to pray for her request. As you may have guessed, I receive excellent personal attention and service in first class that day.

Divine Appointments Principle #24:
*Some divine appointments are too obvious to miss.*

## CHAPTER 31

# "I CAN'T BELIEVE WHAT I JUST SAW"

I am returning home from a meeting, driving west on I-69 through Flint, Michigan. I have just passed under Saginaw Street, and I am directly behind a small compact car.

Suddenly, the rear wheel on the driver's side on the compact car becomes detached, rolls across the two westbound lanes, and hits a concrete wall separating our side of the expressway from the eastbound lanes. Then it shoots straight up in the air and hits an expressway light, bringing the whole assembly down onto the passing lane. The compact car skids to the side of the expressway. Fortunately, I safely steer between the compact car and the fallen light assembly. I pull off to the side of the expressway and walk back to the compact to make sure everyone in the other car is not hurt. I can't believe what I just saw happen.

Lee, the driver, is assessing the damage. He is already making a call on his cell phone by the time I arrive. When he hangs up, I explain to him what I saw as his rear tire became a "pinball" and caromed all over the highway. I help him retrieve his tire.

Before I leave, I ask him what I can be praying for him. He is on his way to a job interview, and he would like God to reschedule it. I assure him that I will be praying.

As I drive off, I am thanking God for keeping all of us safe. I am also thanking Him for giving me a front row seat at some pretty incredible action scenes.

Divine Appointment Principle #25:
*Auto accidents are great places for finding divine appoint-ments. Be a blessing.*

# CHAPTER 32

# "I DON'T BELIEVE IN THIS GOD THING"

**I** am often amazed at remarks from people who attempt to settle their issues with God by denying His existence or avoiding Him altogether. I wonder if they really do believe that He doesn't exist or if they simply don't want to obey Him if he does.

I am attending the National Missionary Convention in Oklahoma. Several of us involved in campus ministry decide to have dinner together one evening. We know each other well and enjoy getting together whenever we can.

Our waitress this evening is a unique blessing. Shy is her name, and she is anything but shy. We are having a good time joking around with her. I ask her for a prayer request; she responds, "I don't believe in this God thing."

I have been waiting for years for a statement like that from a divine appointment. I explain to her, "You don't have to believe in God to give us a prayer request. We are the ones praying. We are the ones who need to believe in God, not you."

It must have "struck a chord" with her because she later returns to our table and asks us to pray for her children. God has a way of taming unbelief with love and truth. He is the God of compassion and understanding.

Divine Appointment Principle #26:
*It is not about your divine appointment's faith in God; it is all about yours.*

# CHAPTER 33

# "I DON'T KNOW IF YOU REMEMBER ME"

**I** am at Plymouth State University (PSU) in Plymouth, New Hampshire. A group of staff and students had heard that I was going to be in the state, so they had asked if I would come up to PSU on this Sunday evening to advise them on how to begin a campus ministry on their campus. We enjoy our time together. After I teach at their gathering this evening, they ask me to return in a couple of months and speak to the group on the topic, "Why I Believe There is a God." They want to invite some of their agnostic and atheist friends to the meeting to hear the teaching.

On my second visit, I am surprised that several of their non-believing friends are in attendance at the meeting. I teach on "Why I Believe There is a God," and many of the non-believers stay around after the meeting.

I strike up a conversation with a male student who identifies himself as an agnostic. We are having a good conversation together when God just prompts me with a challenge for the agnostic. I tell him, "You know, if you're right about God, and I'm wrong, no big deal. But if I'm right and you're wrong, you're in a lot of trouble. I want you to consider something. Pray for two weeks as if there is a God, and ask Him to reveal Himself to you. If after two weeks He hasn't revealed Himself to you, then you're right, and I'm wrong. If he does reveal Himself to you, then do something about it."

The man confidently responds, "I can do that."

I give him my business card and tell him that I would like to hear what happens; he says that he will let me know.

I don't hear from him right away. About six months later I am in my office one morning, when the phone rings. I answer it, but no one responds. All I can hear is sobbing. I assume that this is a fairly significant phone call, so I decide that I should wait until the person composes himself. Finally he says, "I don't know if you remember me, but I am the agnostic you met at Plymouth State University a few months ago. I did what you suggested about praying to God and asking Him to reveal Himself to me. God has continually revealed Himself to me ever since we talked. I am ready to become a Christian. What should I do?"

My power is nothing when compared to God's power. I am so humbled by that thought. He is totally worthy of ceaseless praise from my lips.

Divine Appointment Principle #27:
*Don't be afraid to let God prove Himself.*

# CHAPTER 34

# "I REMEMBER WHERE I HEARD YOUR NAME"

Our campus ministry is considering starting a campus ministry somewhere in Colorado. Whenever we come to the point of determining where, we will send a prayer team to that site for a few days to pray and listen to what God might communicate to us.

We decide to send a prayer team to Boulder and see if God wants us to begin a ministry at the University of Colorado. Five of us are going to be on the prayer team. I start researching what campus ministries are already there in order to meet with one or two of them during our time on campus to receive their input. When I look at the university's web site, I find several Christian groups. I select Christian Challenge and contact the campus minister, Bobby Pruett.

I tell him who I am and ask if he can meet our prayer team on campus to share with us what God is doing. He graciously agrees to do so. He then tells me that my name is familiar, but neither of us can figure out where we have met before.

Our prayer team flies into Denver; then we drive up to Boulder. We spend some time praying over the campus and over the city. Later we meet Bobby on campus; again he is very gracious and extremely helpful.

As we are leaving the meeting, he pulls me aside and tells me, "I remembered where I heard your name. You led a workshop on journaling at an Ivy Jungle Conference a while ago, and I purchased the recording and transcribed it into a file. That teaching has so blessed my life." (This teaching is now available by pod cast at www.deantrune.com.)

I am astounded at how God brings people together for the purpose of blessing one another. He recognizes our need for support and encouragement. I continue to intercede for the Bobby and his family.

Divine Appointment Principle #28:
*God knows how to grant us favor with divine appointments from other ministries (even ahead of time).*

CHAPTER 35

# "I SAW YOU READING YOUR BIBLE"

I am in the Akron-Canton airport on a Sunday evening, traveling home from leading a seminar at First Christian Church in New Philadelphia, Ohio. I'm tired from the weekend, and I am really looking forward to arriving home.

I am sitting at my gate. A lady enters the gate area and sits down two chairs from me. She pulls out her Bible and begins reading. I do not see that often in airports, so it captures my interest.

The gate agent interrupts my thought by announcing that it is time to begin boarding our flight to Detroit. We pick up our carry-on luggage and form a line at the door. I find myself directly behind the "Bible-reading" woman. I sense that a conversation is in order, so I begin, "I saw you reading your Bible. Are you a Christian?" She affirms that she is and introduces herself as Jennifer. This leads to some more conversation as we board our plane.

We connect again as we are deplaning in Detroit. She has a few hours to wait for her flight to Paris, and I have a two-hour layover for my flight to Lansing. She begins to explain to me why she is headed to France to visit her uncle. He has had a heart attack, and he is not a Christian. She wants to be there when he comes out of his coma to be able to talk to him about Jesus.

I am impressed with her courage and her sensitivity to God. She explains that our meeting is God's confirmation that she's doing what He desires. We end our conversation after I pray for her and this adventure that God is directing. We exchange contact information, and she promises to let me know what God does in Paris.

At this time, Bonnie and I have about 30 Moses People who pray for each trip and speaking engagement. When I update them on what God has done over the weekend in New Philadelphia, I ask them to pray for Jennifer's trip to Paris. Many of them reply that they will be excited to pray for her. As Jennifer updates me on her trip, I pass along the information to the Moses People.

I am so impressed with God that He brought Jennifer across my path in perfect timing, and He also raised up a group of additional prayer warriors to cover her trip. Even as the years pass, I continue to pray for Jennifer and her husband Blair regularly. We have stayed in touch through e-mail and Facebook. I have asked her to write her account of our divine appointment, and here it is.

*My Uncle David was transferred and had been working in Paris, France, for several years. One day I received word that he had a sudden heart attack. I was in shock and disbelief because he was only 60 years old, and he kept himself physically fit by walking regularly. He collapsed on the sidewalk after having lunch with a coworker and was in the intensive care unit on a ventilator. My Uncle Jim had immediately flown to Paris, to be with him in the hospital, as he had no other family there. However, after a week he was forced to return to the states for work. As a nurse in cardiology, I knew this was still a critical time for my uncle and that family still needed to be there. I was able to get a week off work to fly out to be with him while he was in the hospital. I believe God still performs miracles, and I wanted to pray for his healing. Initially, to my surprise, I met resistance from my dad and Uncle Jim. They finally gave in, and I scheduled my flight out. I had packed my bag and was determined to fly to Paris to pray for my Uncle David; however, as the time for me to leave came nearer, I became more and more anxious. I was going to a foreign country where I didn't speak the language, didn't know my way around, didn't have an international cell phone, and didn't really know anyone in France except for one of my uncle's co-workers that I had met a few years back. After flying overseas and arriving the next day due to the time change, I planned to take a taxicab from the airport to the hospital to meet Uncle Jim. After that, Uncle Jim would show me how to get to Uncle David's apartment, where I would stay. He would then fly back to the US. I wondered if maybe God didn't want me to go, and that's why my family put up such a fuss initially. Maybe this was my own idea.*

*I was in the Akron/Canton airport, feeling very anxious, waiting to fly to Detroit, then on to Paris. I decided to read my Bible. I was wondering if I was doing the right thing and felt like I could cry. I prayed for confirmation from God that I was doing the right thing. I put my Bible down, and a man started talking to me. As a single woman, I did not typically talk to people I didn't know, and never in detail about my travel plans; therefore, I usually do not meet people in airports. This man started talking to me about the Bible. I tried to keep to myself, but as a Christian I did not want to miss an opportunity to talk to someone about the Bible. It turns out this man, Dean, was a Christian. He was sincere and very kind. I really needed someone to be kind to me at that time. It took me a while to open up, but I was able to tell him about my Uncle David. Dean prayed for me. God used Dean to confirm that I was doing the right thing. Talk about divine timing! God met me right where I was. I went on to*

107

*Paris with a renewed sense of purpose and peace. I was able to pray for my Uncle Dave, who recovered enough that he was transferred to a regular medical floor the week I was there. By the time I was to return home, I knew he would be transferred to a rehabilitation facility within a matter of days. God is good, and He is still a miracle-working God. He will meet you where you are.*

We serve an all-powerful God who not only leads us into obedience but also gives us confirmation along the way. He is indescribably great!

Divine Appointment Principle #29:
*God knows how to use us to affirm others' obedience.*

# CHAPTER 36

# "I'M GLAD I CAME ANYWAY"

Have you ever noticed that often God orchestrates divine appointments to give us a message?

I am leading a "Going Deeper with God" seminar at First Christian Church in Clearwater, Florida. I am preaching in both Sunday morning services and teaching a Sunday school class between them.

People respond very well in the first service, and I have an opportunity to pray with several of them. I teach the Sunday school class, and then I preach in the second service. Again people respond well, and I have more opportunities to pray with people. It is a good day for the Kingdom.

After the second service is over, a woman approaches me and says, "I am so glad I came anyway." This is a little confusing for me, so I ask her to explain.

She says that she was in a restaurant that morning before she came to the church building for the second service. At the restaurant, she ran into a woman she knew who had attended the first service. The woman told her, "We have a guest speaker today, and he is not very good. I wouldn't go if I were you."

I just have to smile. God is reminding me with this divine appointment not to take any credit for what He did that morning. It worked.

Divine Appointment Principle #30:
*God knows how to use divine appointments to teach us character and humility.*

CHAPTER 37

# "I'M MEETING MY HUSBAND AT THE AIRPORT"

I am flying back into Lansing after traveling for a few days. I am tired, and I can't wait to arrive home. I have been upgraded to first class on the short flight from Detroit to Lansing. I am in 2B; I begin to chat with the lady in 2A, whose name is Jen.

I finally ask her what I can be praying for her. She explains that she walked out on her husband a few weeks ago. He called her this weekend and asked her to return to Michigan so they can discuss their marriage face-to-face. Then she says, "I'm meeting my husband at the airport."

I assure her that I will be praying. I am thinking, "What awesome timing on God's part to have me interceding for them both when they meet." While waiting in baggage claim, I observe them talking quietly off to the side of the room, and I am just pouring my heart out to God for Him to bring about restoration and healing.

I am amazed at God's ability to raise up intercessors for us at critical moments in our lives. He is so precise and sensitive to our immediate needs!

Divine Appointment Principle #31:
*God will bring divine appointments into our lives at critical moments in their lives.*

# CHAPTER 38

# IN THE MIDDLE OF YARD WORK

**R**aking leaves is not one of my favorite things to do. In fact, it is not on my "top one million favorite things to do" list. So on this beautiful Michigan fall afternoon, I am begrudging the fact that I need to remove a couple of truckloads of leaves from my front yard.

Fortunately for me, raking leaves is not a function that requires my full attention. Can you really mess up raking leaves? No way. I like the progress of completing a job, but raking leaves is a very boring one.

On this particular day, the weather is perfect, the leaves are deep, and the motivation is low. My bemoaning is interrupted when a construction truck pulls up in front of my house, and the driver rolls down his window to ask me about an address. He needs to make a delivery but is not sure where the property is located. It turns out to be the address of my neighbor who lives across the street and one house south. The deliveryman thanks me and drives off down the street.

As the truck drives away, the thought strikes me that the deliveryman is a divine appointment, and I just missed it. I hate it when that happens! He parks in the neighbor's drive and begins unloading his equipment. Five minutes later, I notice that he is walking down the street toward me. I purpose not to miss this divine appointment. He approaches and tells me that my neighbor is not home. He asks me to give my neighbor the message that he will be back Monday morning to begin the remodeling project; I agree to do so. As he is walking away, I ask him for his first name and if there is anything that I can be praying for him. He pauses and says, "My name is David, and you can pray that I stop drinking." I tell him that I will.

How awesome is that? In the middle of a boring task, God twice brings a divine appointment right to my front yard. Even though I missed it the first time, He gave me another chance. Our great God is so very gracious!

Divine Appointment Principle #32:
*Sometimes God provides a second chance at a divine appointment when we miss the first one.*

CHAPTER **39**

# "IS THERE SOMETHING ELSE WE SHOULD BE PRAYING FOR YOU?"

**I** am spending a couple of days with Kent Smith, a friend of mine in west Texas. He is a professor at Abilene Christian University. On my last night in town, he offers to expose me to some west Texas cuisine. I reply, "Great. What is west Texas cuisine?"

He answers, "Catfish!"

So we drive across Abilene to his favorite catfish place, called Cahoots. We enter the restaurant and are seated in Dee's section. She comes up to our table and introduces herself. She delivers our drinks and takes our order. I ask her if there is something in her life that we can be praying for her. She thinks for a moment, and then says that we can be praying for her parents' visit to campus next year. We say that we will pray. We also discover that she is a student at Abilene Christian University. Even though Kent is a professor there, he and Dee don't know one another; the university is a big place.

After she leaves, I have a sense from God that there is something far more important for us to be praying for Dee. So when she returns to our table, I ask her, "Is there something else we should be praying for you?"

She responds, "You mean like a problem?"

I answer, "That would qualify."

She explains that there is something else, but she is not sure if she wants to share it with us; she will think about it.

After some more trips back to our table, she tells us that she will write down her request and give it to us later as we are leaving the restaurant. We say that will be fine.

As we are leaving the restaurant, she walks up and hands me a note. I tell her "Thanks! We will be praying for you."

As I get in Kent's car in the parking lot, I open the note and read it. She has written the following:

*"I am a senior at ACU, and I am farther from God than I have ever been. Please pray that I can find my way back to Him. Thanks for your prayers."*

I am totally impressed with God. We could have eaten in a hundred different restaurants around Abilene that evening. We could have had fifteen different waitresses or waiters that night, but God immediately led us to Dee. I do not know what God did in Dee's life, but I do know that she was covered in prayer. God has this tremendous ability to bring people across our paths so that we may have the privilege of interceding for them. He is amazing.

Divine Appointment Principle #33:
*Sometimes we have to probe beneath the surface to discover the real need to be praying for in a divine appointment's life.*

# CHAPTER 40

# MAY

Nel and Mindy Go are meeting with me in a Taco Bell® one Sunday for lunch. We have scheduled a marriage check-up for their first year of marriage. We have to wait at the counter for our food for a short while, so we are talking with the cashier named May. She is pleasant, and she appears to be of Middle Eastern descent. Our food finally comes, and we sit down at a table. Just before we finish our review, May takes her break and sits down a few tables over from us. I notice that she bows her head before she begins to eat her meal. As we are leaving, we decide to stop and ask her for a prayer request. Her request is that her family will accept her. Her family is Muslim, and she has made a decision to become a Christian. The conversation really grabs my heart. We tell her we will be praying for her.

The restaurant is located two hours from where I live. As I am driving home, I can't get May out of my mind. I can't imagine what it would be like to have my family disown me because of my Christian faith.

I travel through that city again a couple of weeks later and decide to stop and see how May is doing. I want to ask her some questions about how she became a Christian. She is not working today, so I leave my business card with her boss and ask her to have May call me. I do not hear from her.

After a month of waiting and praying, I contact a friend of Bonnie's and mine who lives in that city. Wendy has a great interest in international people; especially international women. I tell Wendy about the divine appointment with

May and ask her to visit the Taco Bell™ to see if she can make contact with May. Wendy and May become acquainted; over the next few weeks they become great friends. Wendy gives me May's phone number, and I call her to see how we can encourage her. (Wendy told me later that May did not call me when her boss gave her my card because she didn't know who I was, and she thought that I just wanted to have a date with her.)

May did not have a church home, and over the years, Wendy's church has been a tremendous blessing to May.

God continues to work. One day Wendy introduces May to Kathy, who becomes May's second mother and mentor in the faith. May grows quickly. Her favorite thing to do in her free time is to go on the Internet and chat with Muslims about Jesus. She is passionate about reaching her people for Jesus.

I am so impressed with what God can do through a single divine appointment.

Divine Appointment Principle #34:
*God knows how to connect some of my divine appointments with my friends in order for Him to receive the greatest glory.*

# CHAPTER 41

# "MY SISTER ALSO WORKS HERE"

I am having dinner at Shepherd's® in Clearwater, Florida, with someone who wants to assist us in locating some funding for a campus ministry in the area.

Our waitress tonight is Sue; she is taking good care of us. I ask her for a prayer request, and she asks us to be praying for her mother, who has cancer. Sue is touched and overwhelmed by our concern for her, that we care enough to ask for a prayer request. In fact, she sits down at our table and cries. Wow! It is a powerful time of ministry.

When she composes herself, she says, "My sister also works here at Shepherd's®. If I bring her over here, will you also ask her for a prayer request?" We assure her that we will.

Sue brings her sister, Kelly, over to our table and introduces her. When we ask Kelly for a prayer request, she tearfully tells us about her boyfriend Mitch's brain tumor. We commit to pray. I am struck with all the emotional pain in this family and so grateful to God for allowing me to intercede for them.

Almost twelve months after my encounter with Sue and Kelly, I am back in Clearwater, so I decide to revisit Shepherd's® for the express purpose of obtaining an update. Sue is not working this evening, but Kelly is. She gives me the great news that Mitch is doing fine, and life has returned nearly to normal for him. Kelly and Sue's mom continues to struggle with her cancer.

Kelly is grateful that I checked back with her, and I commit to continue to pray.

I wonder how often Christians dine at restaurants and have waitresses or waiters who are hurting deeply. We never discover their pain because, typically, instead of asking questions of concern, we make demands for service. I will never forget Sue and Kelly, and I choose to live a lifestyle in which I always try to find out something that I can be praying for the wait staff.

Divine Appointment Principle #35:
*Some divine appointments look fine on the outside but are hurting deeply on the inside. We need to care enough to ask for a prayer request.*

# CHAPTER 42

# NATION OF ISLAM

**M**y first exposure to the Nation of Islam\*, led by Louis Farrakhan, was on campus at Michigan State University when I was a campus minister there around 1990. I didn't attend his lecture, but I heard much about it. It was woven with hatred toward white people. It was then that I purposed to pray for Mr. Farrakhan and his organization. In my journal I have them listed on Tuesday, Thursday, and Saturday. (My journal is detailed in my first book, *The Path Toward Passion*, Prayershop Publishing 2009.) God is so good at bringing people across our path for whom we are interceding. Here is one example.

I am flying out of Sacramento very early this morning. The airport shuttle, a large sixteen-passenger van, arrives at my hotel. The driver is the only one in it, so I decide to ride in the front passenger seat next to him. We start talking, and I learn that his name is Michael. We stop at other hotels, but no one else boards our van.

I ask Michael if there is something that I can be praying for him, and he responds, "Pray that I get more serious about my God."

I am impressed with his prayer request, so I ask him what his religion is. He says, "I'm a member of the Nation of Islam."

I question him further, "Really? Louis Farrakhan."

He looks at me oddly and asks, "You know about the Nation of Islam?"

I answer, "I pray for Louis Farrakhan and the Nation of Islam three times each week." I don't tell Michael what I pray; I just mention that I pray.

Michael is both surprised and impressed, I think. We have a great conversation in his van, and as we stop at my terminal, I tell him that I want to pray for him right now. I reach over, put my hand on his shoulder, and pray for him to connect with God.

As I am flying home, I am thinking about how impressed I am with God bringing Michael across my path and giving me an opportunity to pray for him. Once home, I decide that I want to buy Michael a gift. I go to a Christian bookstore and buy him a copy of Josh McDowell's book, *More Than a Carpenter*. I contact the hotel to find out what Michael's last name is. I write on the inside cover, "Michael, This is my God." I sign it and mail it to the hotel under Michael's name.

I don't know what God has done in Michael's life, but I know that I was obedient to what God led me to do. Our God is a great God, and He is worth knowing personally. This is one divine appointment that I am glad I did not miss. Our God is glorious.

Divine Appointment Principle #36:
*If we are serious about interceding for a group of people, God can orchestrate a divine appointment with someone from that group. He is amazing.*

*The **Nation of Islam** is an African-American religious movement founded in Detroit, Michigan, by Wallace D. Fard Muhammad in July, 1930. He set out to improve the spiritual, mental, social, and economic condition of the black men and women of America.

# CHAPTER 43

# "OLIVE GARDEN®?"

Bonnie's favorite place to eat out is the Olive Garden®; she loves anything Italian. There is an Olive Garden® within two miles of where we live in Okemos. We eat there several times each year.

It is our thirty-fifth wedding anniversary, so I suggest that the two of us go out to eat. She responds enthusiastically, "Let's go to Olive Garden®!"

I ask, "Olive Garden®? Are you sure?" The reason I am questioning her is not that I do not like the food there; I just don't like the prayer requests. On a recent visit, we asked our waiter, Chris, for a prayer request, and he said that he didn't have one because prayer was a private matter. Since I know that Bonnie really wants to go, I give in, and we drive to her favorite restaurant.

We are seated in a quiet section of the restaurant. Duane approaches our table, introduces himself, and explains that he is our waiter tonight. (I am relieved that it's not Chris.) After he takes our order, he asks if there is anything else. I explain to him that we always look for something to pray about in our waiter's life; I ask him to give it some thought and let us know before we leave. He responds, "I don't have to wait. I already know what you can be praying for me." (Now I am really liking this guy.) He continues, "My two daughters live with their mom in Muskegon, and I hardly ever see them. Pray for them and that I will be able to see them more often. Their names are Lydia and Abigail." We assure Duane that we will pray, and he goes into the kitchen to turn in our order.

Within a few minutes, Duane returns with pictures of Lydia and Abigail, saying, "Since you are going to pray for them, you might as well know what they look like." He is delighted that we want to pray for his daughters. My love for the Olive Garden® is slowly being resurrected.

Bonnie and I thoroughly enjoy our time together and our time with Duane. As we leave the restaurant, I am thinking what a great blessing God has given us tonight in having Duane as our waiter. The divine appointment has been a great wedding anniversary gift from God.

Two months later, Bonnie and I decide to eat out, and once again she chooses the Olive Garden®. I am less resistant this time because of our divine appointment with Duane. As we walk into the restaurant, I suggest that we request to sit in Duane's section if he is working tonight. She nixes that idea, so we will just wait to see who God provides for our divine appointment.

Our waitress this evening is Lisa. She is very nice and we have a great time chatting with her. She is a Christian; her prayer request is that we pray for direction in her life concerning a job. We agree to pray for that specific prayer request.

Lisa is gone for a few minutes when Duane shows up at our table. He is so excited to see us again, and he gives us an update on his daughters. He says that he was standing next to the servers' workstation, and Lisa was telling him about this couple who asked her for a prayer request. He says that he knew right away that we were the couple. He had to come out and talk with us. (I am now really beginning to like the Olive Garden®.) I love it when God blesses others through Bonnie and me. When we simply care enough about people to find out what we can be praying for them, God can show up in powerful ways. He is so good!

Divine Appointment Principle #37:
*Not everyone will respond well to being a divine appointment. That is no reason to stop looking for them.*

# CHAPTER 44

# PERFECT TIMING

Many times I have experienced divine appointments in which the person is anxious for good reasons. I will share three such divine appointments, where God is walking individuals through tough times.

**Emergency surgery:**

I am on an early flight out of Lansing to Minneapolis. The morning has been a big rush to arrive at the airport in time to catch my flight. I have been upgraded to first class; I am seated in 1B.

I introduce myself to my seatmate in 1A. Her name is Diane, and she can't seem to relax. We have been talking for a while when I finally ask what I can be praying for her.

She responds, "As we speak, my husband is having surgery in Dallas, and I am here in Michigan visiting friends. I received a call last night that I needed to return home as soon as possible because my husband was having emergency surgery this morning. Please pray that surgery will go well and that I can be with him when he wakes up in recovery."

I assure her that I will be praying, and I am so impressed that God put me next to someone who needs prayer at this very moment.

**Daughter-in-law dying:**

I am flying from Lansing to Minneapolis on an early flight. I am seated next to Ruth, a lady who seems to be very much consumed with her thoughts. We chat for a while; then I asked her what I can be praying for her. Ruth explains that her daughter-in-law has been given one week to live, so Ruth is flying out to California to be with her until she dies.

I can't imagine the pain that lies ahead for this lady, but I am humbled that God is giving me the opportunity to intercede for her in this very difficult time.

**Father passing:**
I am flying into Chicago; I have been upgraded to first class. I am sitting in 4B, but I just can't seem to get a conversation started with the gentleman in 4A. He is very anxious. He reads a couple of pages in a book, then puts it down. He nervously pulls out the airline magazine, flips through a few pages, and then puts it away. At times he just stares out the window, apparently deep in thought.

Finally I am able to begin a conversation. His name is Mike. We chat for a while before I ask him what I can be praying for him. He responds in surprise, "I can't believe that you are asking me that question. I am on my way to see my father, who lives in Chicago. He has been given just this weekend to live. I am going to be with him until he dies. Please be praying for us. This is not going to be easy."

Again I am so privileged for God to placed me next to someone who needs intercession right now. Our God is so good!

Divine Appointment Principle #38:
*When people are experiencing overwhelming sorrow and distress, God sends intercessors to love them and pray for them at their moment of greatest need.*

# CHAPTER 45

# PROSTITUTES AND SALT LAKE CITY

I am on campus at Central Christian College of the Bible in Moberly, Missouri. I am here this week speaking on spiritual renewal. I have spent time speaking in chapel each day, and I have taught in several classes on a variety of topics. Right now I am looking for a place to sit down and study. I make my way to the cafeteria (their version of a student union). I like this place. I have enjoyed several good conversations with students and have appreciated the "missional" atmosphere.

I sit down at a table where two students are studying. I am not looking for a conversation, but Nicole begins speaking to me. We are chatting about general things as she explains that she is originally from the state of Washington but ended up spending some time in Salt Lake City. I have led prayer journeys to Salt Lake City several times, so I ask her about her time there. As Nicole is sharing her story, I am thinking that this is a great divine appointment with Nicole about an incredible divine appointment she had. Here is her story.

*One night as I was leaving work, I got a call from a friend who was at a bar and had decided that he'd had too much to drink; he needed a ride home. Once I figured out where he was, I headed into downtown Salt Lake and picked him up, managing to get him home after about 45 minutes of driving to find an apartment that was six blocks away from where we had started.*

*While walking back to my car, I was approached by a... woman of negotiable affections, a prostitute. She wanted to know if I would like some company for a couple of hours. I think it surprised both of us when I said yes. Don't get me wrong. I didn't say yes for the reason people normally say yes to prostitutes, but I just felt led to say "Yes."*

*"What do you want to do, sugar?" she asked me.*

*I looked around, a little wide-eyed, I'm sure.*

*"Are you hungry?" I asked.*

*She said she was.*

*"Do you mind if I buy you some dinner then, and maybe we can talk for a while?"*

*She looked at me like I had horns growing out of my forehead, but nodded, "It's your dime..."*

*At Denny's™ (thank God for 24-hour diners!) she told me her name was Divine and that she was 26 years old, originally from Nashville, Tennessee. Divine was good-looking in a tired way ... obviously beautiful at one time. I think if she hadn't been on the street for the better part of a decade, she could have been a model.*

*But there are enough shoulda-coulda's in Divine's life already, and that's just one more she'd prefer not to think about.*

*She could have been a mother three times, but she aborted the babies. She thinks about those three decisions a lot.*

*She could have been a murder victim, but she got lucky one night. She thinks a lot about that, too.*

*She could have been loved by somebody, but she doesn't deserve that anymore. She thinks mostly about that.*

*When Divine said that last bit, about not being worthy of love, I reached out and grabbed her hand, and without even thinking, said, "I love you."*

*Divine laughed.*

*"Sugar, you don't even know me."*

*"No," I said, "but I still love you. Because you're a fellow human, a fellow woman, and one of God's amazing creations. That's enough reason right there for me to love you."*

*Divine looked at me, skeptical. "Let me guess... next you're gonna tell me that you got some friends that wanna love me tonight, too?"*

*This time I laughed. "Nope. Just me. Just dinner, and I'm paying."*

*Divine leaned back in her seat. "So, are you one of those weird religious freaks?"*

*I laughed, and, shaking my head, replied, "I love Jesus."*

*"Oh," she said. "So what's life like on the Jesus train?" I told her about when I became a believer, how the only option for me that night was to kill myself or put my life in God's hands. I told her about struggling with the reality of rape and the fallout that caused after I recovered from it. I told her*

about a lot of difficult stuff that I've gone through, and that the only reason I got through it is that I knew there was Someone who loved me unconditionally. God was the only thing that got me through.

And then I told her about a lot of the good things that have happened to me and how I purposed to be faithful to God. He rewards faithfulness. Sometimes He just gives me good times, not because I deserve them, but because it's His way of saying "I still love you."

Divine looked up at me from across the table and said with a tear in her eye, "So... you're God's way of telling me He still loves me...?"

I smiled. "Yeah. God loves you, and so do I."

Divine and I talked until 7 AM. We ended up having dinner AND breakfast. I shared Jesus with her in the most real and organic way I knew how. I told her of how much He loves her and how He wants to be able to love on her for all eternity. She didn't decide right then to give her life over to Him, but I could see it in her... she's thinking about it.

When we were ready to leave, I prayed for Divine and asked for God's special protection for her, His healing in her life, and His grace to abound. I gave her my phone number and told her anytime she wants to hop on the Jesus train to give me a call.

By the end of that summer, due to God's grace and obedience on the part of the people's lives in whom He works, I was privileged to witness to more than two hundred women stuck in lives of prostitution, twenty-eight of whom I had the honor

132

*of baptizing into a saving relationship with our Lord. Divine was one of the twenty-eight.*

As I have read and reread Nicole's story, I am over-whelmed with the thought that unconditional love impacts people's hearts deeply. There is hope for any wandering person to find Jesus: even in a "Divine" appointment. Our God is beautifully amazing.

Divine Appointment Principle #39:
*No one is outside of God's reach. Just love them unconditionally.*

# CHAPTER 46

# "READY TO GIVE UP ON MY MARRIAGE"

I am flying into Baltimore to lead a seminar at a church in Fork, Maryland, for the weekend. It is my second or third time at this particular church. I enjoy the minister and his family very much. I have made some friends in the congregation on my previous visits. I am looking forward to the weekend.

On Saturday evening we decide to eat out, so the minister, his family, and I choose to eat at a local buffet. It is fun, and the food is great. Back at home later that evening, we coordinate our plans for the morning. We will eat breakfast at a particular time, and I will speak at the 9 AM and 11 AM services. It is going to be an enjoyably day.

In the middle of the night, I wake up deathly sick. As I am waiting to throw up one more time, I just try to listen to God. He prompts me with the idea that someone will be in one of the morning services who is "ready to give up on her marriage." He wants me to be ready to pray with her. I am not even sure that I am going to be in the services myself, but I hear what He says.

I have been up for at least two hours; I am finally beginning to think I can go back to bed. I leave a note on the dining room table explaining that I am sick, so I won't need anything for breakfast. I will be at the church in time to preach in the first service.

I haul myself out of bed after 8 AM and begin getting ready to go to the church building. Food is not an option this morning. I am just praying to make it through the morning without embarrassing God or myself. I preach for the first service and offer an invitation. I mention that someone may be in this service who is ready to give up a marriage. Some people step forward, and I pray with them, but there isn't anyone who is ready to give up on a marriage. I assume that I must have been delusional during my sickness the night before and that I did not hear God correctly.

After a short rest, I preach in the second service. I offer an invitation but do not mention anything about someone giving up on a marriage. The very first person to respond to the invitation is a woman in tears. She asks me to pray for her; I ask her what I should pray. She explains, "I am ready to give up on my marriage." I am blown away by God's grace as I pray for her and encourage her.

God uses this morning to remind me of an important lesson. In the midst of my wimpiest, weakest, "I-don't-want-to-show-up" times, He is still powerful enough to accomplish things in spite of me. He doesn't need me at my best. He simply needs me to "show up." We serve an amazing God!

Divine Appointment Principle #40:
*In spite of me not being at my best, God can still work supernaturally through me. It is all about His abilities, not mine.*

# CHAPTER 47

# REKA AND ZANE

Bonnie and I are visiting our son, Ryan, and his wife, Reka, in Phoenix for Christmas. This Christmas is special because it is their son Zane's first one. Reka is originally from Hungary; Ryan met her while he was in Medical School in Szeged. The day before our return to Michigan, Reka is scheduled to fly to Hungary to visit her parents. She is a little concerned because she is traveling with Zane, who at this time is three and a half months old. The trip to Budapest will include two flights with a four-hour layover in London's Heathrow Airport. The total travel time will be nineteen hours.

She expresses her concern, and I assure her, "God will send angels if you need help." Both Bonnie and I commit to be praying for her trip.

Here is Reka's account of her trip.

*On the flight from Phoenix to London, I sat next to a lady who initially seemed annoyed that she had a seat next to a baby. After takeoff she seemed to warm up to us and thought that Zane was a good distraction for her since she had suffered from anxiety at takeoff.*

*She turned out to be a great help because of her connection to the pilot. The British Airways® people in Phoenix told me that I could not retrieve my stroller at the Heathrow airport, even though we had the four-hour layover. She asked the pilot to take care of it, and he did. When we exited the plane in London, our stroller was waiting for us.*

*Also, on the first flight, I heard a lady speaking angrily to her daughter in Hungarian, and I mentioned to her that I understood what she was saying. She waited for me to exit the plane in London because I think she was embarrassed that I knew what she was really saying to her daughter. We spent the whole four hours at Heathrow together and were scheduled on the same flight to Budapest. My time at Heathrow would have been a lot harder without them. She and her daughter fell in love with Zane. They watched him while I used the rest room and greatly helped in his care.*

*At baggage claim in Budapest, she loaded my cart while I held on to Zane. Overall, she was a tremendous blessing. Afterward, I wanted to send a thank you gift, but all I had was her first name. At Heathrow, I had written my e-mail address on a piece of paper for her. My e-mail address contains both my first and last name. Four months later she contacted me on Facebook, and I was able to obtain the information necessary to send her daughter a thank you gift. We have plans to get together on my next trip to Hungary.*

When Reka e-mailed me these stories, I was convinced that God had sent two angels (or at least two divine appointments) to assist her on the trip. Reka also believes that God sent these two women. What an amazing God we serve! *"Because of the Lord's great love we are not consumed, for His compassions never fail. They are new every morning; great is your faithfulness."* Lamentations 3:22-23

Divine Appointment Principle #41:
*We can even pray divine appointments into existence.*

CHAPTER 48

# "SHE SHOULDN'T BE DATING HIM"

I am heading home from Rochester, Minnesota, one morning. I have just finished spending a few days on a Bible college campus leading a spiritual renewal time. It has been an incredible experience as students have spent hours repenting and confessing sin in their lives. I am on a flight from Minneapolis to Detroit.

Cathy, across the aisle from me, works for the airline and is commuting to work. She is a flight attendant, and she is telling me about her life. She identifies herself as a Christian and describes the vibrant church she attends. She also describes the man she is currently dating. She is a single mom who has never been married. As she is describing her boyfriend, Scott, to me, all I can think is, "She shouldn't be dating him because he is not a spiritual leader to her."

I want to tell her, but I don't think I have enough relational capital with her yet since I have only known her for twenty minutes. I feel prompted to offer her a set of teachings by a friend of mine, Randy Gariss, out of Joplin, Missouri. Randy has some powerful material on "Why Marriages Fail," "Why Marriages Work," and "The Differences Between Men and Women." I offer to mail her a set; she says she would appreciate having the materials. I commit to pray for her and to send the teachings to her.

I mail the teachings to her within the next few days. I don't hear from her right away, so I have no idea what God is doing. About six months later I receive a phone call that starts out, "I don't know if you remember me, but we sat next to one another on an airplane a few months ago. You sent me a set of teachings about marriage. I really appreciated them. I broke off the relationship with Scott, and I wanted to let you know. Thanks."

We chat for a while, and she asks to have her name added to our mailing list. A few years later, she is flying into Anchorage one Wednesday evening, and she notices on my schedule (included in the newsletter) that I am speaking at a church in Anchorage this evening. She contacts the church office; someone there puts her in touch with me. Some friends and I pick her up at the airport, and we all have dinner before the service. It is great to see her again after a few years.

Two years later Cathy reads in our newsletter that I am leading Prayer Gatherings in various places. She decides to participate in one in Salt Lake City. The time spent in Utah gives me the opportunity to see how God is growing and using this woman of His.

I want you to hear Cathy's side of the this story.

*I will never forget my divine appointment with Dean!*

*At that time, it opened up my eyes to something I wasn't totally in touch with. God puts people in our pathways for a reason! This appointment was a pivotal time in my life for both my spiritual walk and for the direction God wanted me to go in my future.*

*Somewhere in my heart I knew Dean was a messenger from God. As I remember, I believe God had already been speaking to me for a while to get out of the relationship I was in. Dean was right on and just another confirmation. Our flight into Detroit was delayed, so I had more time with Dean. He prayed for me on the plane. During this prayer time I remem-*

140

*ber being very moved by the presence of the Holy Spirit. It almost was as if no one else was on the plane!*

*I had one other relationship with a man named Jon before I met my husband. He and I thought we were supposed to be together as he was a pretty strong Christian, also had never been married, and wanted kids. But, as divine appointments continued in my life, people were put in my path to let me know differently. Three different people who did not know each other prophesied to Jon at different times that we were not supposed to be together. It was confusing for us at the time, but, again, I knew in my heart that this was right. God even put another person, someone who knew of Jon but who was a complete stranger to me, on a flight to confirm another message.*

*You see, God had me headed toward my wonderful husband, Paul! So, with many more of God's divine appointments and confirmations, I met my husband on a mission trip. This time I knew in my heart, as he did, that we were supposed to be together, but we didn't tell each other. We just asked God separately to confirm this over and over again. And He did. Unknown to us at that time, He had us reading in the same scripture passage.*

*A few years after we were married, God called us to adopt our wonderful daughter Hannah. Again he set up divine appointments and confirmed that we were supposed to adopt her. Having Hannah share Paul's birthday was a wonderful present from God.*

*Anchorage meeting: I called the church contact's home when I found out Dean was going to be speaking in Anchorage to ask where Dean was staying. To my surprise, she said he was staying with her family and asked if I would like to speak to him as he was right there. The really neat thing about that conference was that the night I attended the church to listen to Dean speak, his topic just so happened to be on DIVINE APPOINTMENTS. That was so fun!*

*Salt Lake City trip: The prayer gathering in Salt Lake with Dean and the rest of the group was wonderful. I especially remember how sweet it was when Dean printed a photo of Hannah, sent from our agent before the adoption was final, that came through to him from Paul. It was very special because I believe it was only the second picture that we had seen of Hannah. I was able to share our adoption process with this awesome group in Salt Lake and receive much needed prayer!*

*I believe God put Dean in my path for many reasons. As I said before, it was a pivotal time in my life to learn about God's divine appointments that have continued in my life and have led me to ministry, my husband, our daughter, and so much more!*

She has a very supportive church family now, a wonderful Christian husband, and beautiful children. I am so impressed at how God is able to bring phenomenal people into our lives through divine appointments and bless us with friendships.

Divine Appointment Principle #42:
*God knows the best way to present truth to our divine appointments.*

# CHAPTER 49

# "SON WORSHIPER?"

**I** arrive at the Seattle airport early this morning for a long flight to Memphis. I am looking for a quiet flight. I had led a seminar at a church over the weekend, and I am tired. I have been upgraded to first class, so I figure that I can get some much-needed sleep. But God has other ideas.

I sit down in 1B and start a conversation with a gentleman in 1A. He explains that he is a contractor in the Seattle area and that he is headed to Memphis on business. After a short while, I ask what I can pray for him over the next month. He responds, "Wow, we need to talk."

We talk most of the way to Memphis. He has questions and wants input on his life. After a while, he suggests that I stop and pray for him right now; I do. It is a great time.

My new friend gets up and goes to the front rest room. As he passes through the front section of the plane, the flight attendant asks him if he is a "Son worshiper." He answers, "Yes." Then the flight attendant approaches me and asks the same question. I assured him that I am. We chat for a minute, and I ask him for a prayer request. He gives me one, then goes back to work.

A short while later he returns to my seat. He explains that his buddy, a flight attendant working in coach this flight, is not a Christian. He asks me, "Hey, if I bring him up here to first class, will you ask him for a request?" I say, "Sure." He brings his friend up to first class; I ask him for a prayer request. We all have a great time, and it becomes one of my most enjoyable flights. I am thinking sleep, and God is thinking divine appointments. He is incredible!

Divine Appointment Principle #43:
*If I focus on my needs and desires, I will typically miss great divine appointments.*

CHAPTER 50

# "THAT'S NOT WHAT WE SHOULD BE PRAYING"

**I** am flying into Oklahoma to lead a seminar at a church I have not visited before. In fact, I have never met David Logsdon, the senior minister, before today. We have only talked on the phone. He picks me up at the airport, and we begin the trip to his city. We decide to eat on the way, so we stop at one of his favorite restaurants.

I don't think David knows our waitress personally, but he knows of her through someone at his church. We ask her for a prayer request; she asks us to pray for her work on her master's degree. After she leaves our table, Dave says, "That's not what we should be praying for her." He explains that there are some issues in her life concerning a boyfriend and a pregnancy that really need prayer.

I add her name to my divine appointment journal, and over the next thirteen months I pray for her each week.

Recently, I received a communication from David telling me that our divine appointment and her former-boyfriend-now-husband have become Christians. There is no way of telling how many divine appointments eventually become Christians, but I think heaven will be full of surprises. We serve a phenomenal God!

Divine Appointment Principle #44:
*Pray for our divine appointments to be "right" with God.*

# CHAPTER 51

# "THIS IS FOR YOU"

I want to tell you more about the time when I was in Abilene, Texas, staying with my friend Kent Smith, who teaches at Abilene Christian University. I told you about the divine appointment we had with Dee at Cahoots back in chapter 39.

I am on my way from Michigan to Los Angeles, and Kent has made plans for me to stop over in Abilene for three days. He has set up some teaching opportunities for me on campus.

It is the middle of the night, but I am wide-awake. Gathering my Bible and my journal, I pray for God to lead me in this time with Him. God first leads me to Ezekiel 4, where God is showing Ezekiel how He wants to symbolize the siege of Jerusalem.

I write in my journal, "At times God requires each of us to be a prophet, regardless of how it appears or if we understand."

Next, He clearly and precisely directs me to Jonah 2:8. I don't know what is in Jonah 2:8, but I am excited to get there and find out. The passage reads:

"Those who cling to worthless idols forfeit the grace that could be theirs."

This verse powerfully hits me. If I cling to worthless idols, grace will not be given to me. I start to think about the worthless idols that life offers us. I begin by writing:

"Some trade the God of Creation–the God of the Universe for the following idols:

- the god of immorality
- the god of pornography
- the god of prayerlessness
- the god of self-centeredness
- the god of pride
- the god of drunkenness
- the god of poor self-worth
- the god of man
- the god of discouragement
- the god of hopelessness

The thoughts just pour out of my mind and into my journal. I write, "You have committed spiritual adultery, and as God reaches out with nail-pierced hands and a tear-stained face, He says, 'I love you; will you take my hand and my heart and walk with me?'"

I begin to wonder how God wants me to act as a prophet, and is this message in Jonah 2:8 for me or for the campus here at ACU? God appears to be stirring my heart to share this message. I am not scheduled to speak again at ACU, and I find out that there is not an opportunity to add any speaking times for me.

This message weighs heavily on my heart, but it apparently has nothing to do with anything in Abilene.

The next day, I board a plane for Los Angeles. I am scheduled to lead a beach retreat for Hope International University in Fullerton over the weekend.

I speak on campus at chapel before heading south of LA for the beach retreat. It is a beautiful location right on the Pacific Ocean. God moves powerfully through our midst for the entire weekend.

On the way back to campus on Sunday afternoon, Priscilla Schubert, the Resident Life Coordinator for Women, asks me if I will meet with one of her resident assistants (RA's). This particular RA was not on the retreat, and she has not been doing well spiritually. When I agree, Priscilla arranges our meeting.

I walk into the residence hall later that night and introduce myself to the RA. She begins to tell me about her life. About twenty minutes into her story, it hits me. She is clinging to worthless idols, and she is suffering as a result. When she finishes, I pull out my journal and tell her, "This is for you." I share with her what God shared with me three nights ago in Abilene, Texas. She begins to weep; she knows that this is God's gentle message for her personally. I see God supernaturally begin a healing process in this young lady's life; I am so grateful for a "front row" seat. I call Priscilla later, and we discuss how she can specifically help this precious child of God.

God overwhelms me with His grace. I am totally amazed at how He will give me a passage and some journaling thoughts that are to be shared with someone I have not met yet, someone who is 1200 miles and four days away. Only God can do this. He is phenomenal! I wonder how many times God has prompted me with something for someone else, but I have dismissed them because I didn't see the opportunity to share them with someone that day.

Divine Appointment Principle #45:
*God can be specifically preparing us for a divine appointment several days in advance. Our responsibility is to be prepared.*

# CHAPTER 52

# "THIS IS NOT ABOUT RENTING A CAR"

We are running a little late; it has been a long day already. I have flown out of Lansing early in the morning and have had a stopover in Minneapolis before flying on to Denver. The plan is for me to meet my friend, David Empson, at the Denver airport. My flight is on time, but David's flight is two hours late. He finally arrives, and we take the car rental shuttle to pick up the car he has reserved.

As we walk into the car rental agency, a customer is just leaving the counter, so we walk right up to the agent. She identifies herself as Ann and asks if we have a reservation. David says he does and gives her the information. She asks what we are doing in the area; we tell her we are attending a Christian conference near Estes Park. She remarks that her dad is a minister and that she did the whole church thing growing up. She also states that she had moved to Denver about three years ago and really enjoys the area. I feel prompted to ask her where she is attending church in the Denver area. She explains that she has not found one yet; my guess is that she has not been looking. She explains that her parents ask her regularly about her church, and she simply tells them that it is great. All of a sudden, I realize that this is a divine appointment, and this is not about renting a car.

She takes us out to the car lot, and we examine our rental for any defects. When she is finished, I explain to her that I believe God has arranged this divine appointment. I ask if we can pray with her before we leave the lot. She says,

"OK," so we have a prayer huddle right there in the parking lot. She is convicted that she needs to look for a church home. I give her my card and ask her to contact me when she finds one; she agrees to do so. I haven't heard from her yet. I simply pray for her, as I do with all divine appointments. I wholeheartedly expect to hear from her someday. God so amazes me with His ability to bring people who need to be prayed for and loved across my path. We can't afford to miss these Kingdom opportunities. I hope to connect with Ann the next time my schedule takes me into Denver.

Divine Appointment Principle #46:
*God will give us the right question to ask our divine appointments. Just listen.*

# CHAPTER 53

# "THIS IS PERFECT TIMING..."

It's January, and I am flying back to Michigan from Florida. I am excited to be heading home after a conference in Florida, but I am not looking forward to the change in weather. My flight from Tampa to Detroit is uneventful. In Detroit, I check the board for my flight to Lansing. I see that it is canceled, as are all the other flights to Lansing.

I check with the airline personnel and am told that the Lansing airport is fogged in; no one knows when the next flight to Lansing will happen. I only live an hour and twenty minutes from the Detroit airport, so I decide to rent a car and drive home.

I catch a shuttle to one of the car rental lots. On the shuttle bus, I start a conversation with Bob, the man sitting next to me. He is renting a car because he needs to attend a meeting in Grand Rapids this evening. He had been scheduled to fly into Lansing and rent a car from there. While we are waiting for service at the lot, I ask him if he would be interested in renting a car together; he can drop me off at my exit as he drives through Lansing. He agrees, and in a short while we are on our way to Lansing. As we are driving along, I ask Bob for a prayer request. He states, "This is perfect timing because my meeting tonight is with my boss, and I am really concerned about it. I don't know if I will have a job when the meeting is over. I definitely need prayer."

Before we turn onto I-96 to head west toward Lansing, my daughter, Kim, calls me on my cell phone and explains that several miles of I-96 are closed because of a massive traffic accident due to the fog. In fact, over one hundred cars are involved, and both sides of the expressway are closed. Since I am familiar with the territory, I am able to direct Bob off the expressway so we can get to Lansing using state roads. He won't let me pay for my half of the rental. He is so excited that I am able to help him arrive at his meeting on time and that his meeting with his boss is being covered in prayer. God orchestrates life well when we follow his lead. He is so good!

Divine Appointment Principle #47:
*When I find myself in the company of a stranger, I can assume that it is a divine appointment.*

# CHAPTER 54

# "WAIT A MINUTE! I HAVE ANOTHER PRAYER REQUEST!"

**I** am attending a conference in Evansville, Indiana, on the campus of Southern Indiana University. Most of the meals are supplied on campus, but one evening we are on our own. Jeff, Tom, Randy, and I decide to try Greek food, and we discover a great place to eat.

As we enter the restaurant, we are greeted by one of the co-owners, Doros. He offers a dinner special to us; for a certain price, he will just keep cooking food and sending it to our table. We accept his offer. He seats us, and Angie, our waitress, starts bringing the food. I ask Angie what we can pray for her; she responds, "Peace of mind." It is an incredible dining experience. We have a great time chatting among ourselves, trying new food, and talking with Angie.

We finish our meal, pay our bill, and are leaving the restaurant when Angie comes running out to stop us, calling, "Wait a minute! I have another prayer request!" She hands us a business card belonging to Doros. She says that Doros's little boy is extremely sick. The doctor does not know for sure what the real problem is, but the family has been called together because they do not know if the little boy is going to survive. We commit to pray, and we thank Angie for both prayer requests.

We pray for Doros's son and for Angie.

The following year, Jeff and I are back at the same conference. On the evening that we are on our own for dinner, we invite two other people to go to dinner with us; we have to return for some more Greek food.

At the restaurant, we ask if Angie is working because we want to be seated in her section. When she comes to our table, we have one happy reunion! She is ecstatic. She points out the table where we had been seated on our previous visit twelve months earlier. She says that Doros is not working this evening, but she is going to contact him and tell him we are back. When he hears that we are in his restaurant, he comes in and sits down at our table. We are all amazed at what is happening but apparently God has been working in Doros's life.

He excitedly shares what God has done for his son. The family was called together, and everyone was expecting the worst. Then, all of a sudden, his son started improving. No one could explain why. His son finally improved enough to be released from the hospital. Now he is completely well and today shows no signs of ever having been sick. Doros looks right at us and says, "I am a blessed man!" He is so appreciative of our prayers. We are overwhelmed with God's goodness.

I have no explanation for why God says "yes" to some prayer requests and "no" to others. He is God, and He is in charge. What I see in this double divine appointment is that people are in awe of our phenomenal God when we give Him an opportunity to move supernaturally. He wants to bless people so that they know that He is doing the blessing. The best part is that He orchestrates our lives so that He can receive the greatest glory. Only God can do that and do that consistently.

Divine Appointment Principle #48:
*When divine appointments see God move supernaturally, they will want to share it with others. God is so powerful!*

CHAPTER **55**

# "WHAT ARE YOU GIVING AWAY TODAY?"

**I** am leading a prayer journey for Northern Plains Evangelistic Association (NPEA) in Laramie, Wyoming. There are about ten of us praying around the city, just seeking what God desires for a church plant. Mike Sojka, who oversees the ministry of NPEA, wants us to spend some time on campus at the University of Wyoming. On this particular day, we are praying around campus; we agree to meet back in the student union around lunchtime to eat and make plans for the afternoon.

We are starting to assemble in the student union, when we discover that there is a student fair taking place there. Several of the student groups on campus have tables set up, and they are either giving away items or providing information about their group.

Some of us on the prayer journey are standing behind a row of tables, talking about some of the student groups we have seen. There is a table near us with three young ladies standing by it. The front of the table is on the other side, so we cannot tell who they are or what they are giving away. I just sense that I need to talk to them. I walk around to the front of the table and ask the question, "What are you giving away today?" Much to my chagrin, they are distributing condoms.

I strike up a conversation with Jen, Sara, and Kara. It is an incredible conversation. I learn that all three are seniors,

159

and they are all nursing students. They are passing out the condoms for Safe Health Week.

I talk to them for about fifteen minutes, and in that time all three tell me that they grew up in church but have not attended one in Laramie since coming to campus. They express an interest in the church that is going to be planted through NPEA. They are honest and gracious. They ask me to pray that they will become involved with spiritual things around Laramie.

As our prayer team moves on from the student union, I am struck by the thought that most students need a connection with someone in order to learn about the spiritual possibilities around a campus. Sometimes that connection shows up in a divine appointment. God knows how to do that.

Divine Appointment Principle #49:
*God knows how to connect us to others in a divine appointment in order to provide a "bridge" for them to return to Him.*

CHAPTER 56

# "WHAT? YOU ARE PLANNING ON BACKPACKING?"

I am returning to the states from a trip to Germany. Three of us are traveling together on a flight from Munich to Amsterdam. My two friends are seated across the aisle from me. I am sitting next to a young lady whose name is Polly. As Polly and I chat, I ask her for a prayer request. She asks me to pray for a safe trip and for her mom not to worry.

I ask her where she is going; she is going to backpack around Mexico for a couple of months. Shocked, I ask, "What? You are planning on backpacking around Mexico?"

Polly responds ruefully, "Yeah, and my mom is a little worried."

We continue to talk about her trip. I ask her, "If you had a Bible, would you read it on your trip?" She said, "Sure."

So I take my Bible out of my backpack, remove some personal papers from it, and write inside the front cover, "May this change your life as much as it has changed mine." She takes it and says that she will read it.

She asks what we are doing in Munich; I explain that my two friends are going to be part of a campus ministry team there. She casually mentions that her ex-boyfriend lives in Munich, and we should contact him because he reads his Bible. She even gives us his name and phone number.

We eat lunch with Polly in the Amsterdam airport and pray with her for a safe trip before heading to our gate for our flight to Detroit.

Several months later, some new members of our Impact team arrive in Munich. One of the women, who was with me when we met Polly, rents an apartment with another lady on the team. They go to a furniture store and purchase some items but then realize that they do not have a way to move the furniture back to their apartment. They called Polly's ex-boyfriend, Thomas, and explaining their predicament and how they received his phone number. He is glad to help and arrives shortly with his pickup truck. It is an amazing divine appointment that results from a previous divine appointment with Polly. The team asks me to be praying regularly for Thomas.

Thomas starts spending time with the team and eventually becomes a Christian. His life is turned "right side up." Thomas and I communicate by e-mail often. About a year after he became a Christian, I have the privilege to meet him in person. We just hug each other for a long time. I am so proud of Thomas. God has even raised him up to do part-time ministry with two different Christian organizations in Munich.

The significance of the divine appointment with Polly did not have much to do with her but had very much to do with Thomas. God is so creative at moving effortlessly among us to connect us with people through other people. He is so phenomenal!

Divine Appointment Principle #50:
*Sometimes God will effortlessly use a divine appointment to pave the way to a second divine appointment.*

# CHAPTER 57

# "WHERE'S JACLYN?"

"Where do you want to eat lunch?" The question is very inviting. I left Michigan very early this morning, flew to Minneapolis, and then on to Seattle. Bill and Corey, two campus ministers, pick me up at the airport; we are spending some time together discussing future ministry plans.

We decide to have lunch at Red Robin®. Jaclyn, our waitress, approaches our table and welcomes us to the restaurant. After she has taken our orders, I explain to her that we always look for something in our waitress's life that we can pray for the next month. I ask her if there is something we can pray for her; she says that she will give it some thought.

When our food arrives, the manager of the restaurant delivers it. I ask the question, "Where's Jaclyn?" She explains that she is covering for Jaclyn because Jaclyn is emotionally unable to bring us our food. Jaclyn is experiencing a very rough year, and our interest in praying for her has touched her heart deeply. Jaclyn is very appreciative but just can't be on the serving floor at the moment. Her prayer request is for guidance.

I didn't expect that. I wonder how often we cross paths with someone who is hurting deeply, but we never "see" it. I give my business card to the manager and offer to assist Jaclyn in any way I can. God really touched my heart with this divine appointment. What a compassionate God we serve!

Divine Appointment Principle #51:
*Don't underestimate how deeply God can impact a divine appointment's heart by being asked for a prayer request.*

# CHAPTER 58

# "WHOA! I HAVE NEVER SEEN THAT BEFORE"

I am at the National Missionary Convention in Indianapolis, having a great time. Some friends of mine from Oceanside, California, Kelly and Mary Margaret Brown, invite me to dinner with some other members of their church. My friends are trying to connect me with their church so God will open a door for me to lead a weekend seminar in Oceanside. (Four years later it happened, and God really blessed it.)

We decide to eat at Champions® near the convention center. Eight of us are seated around a U-shaped booth. Our waiter, Jeremy, takes our orders and asks if there is anything else he can get for us.

I am seated on his right, so I simply ask him if there is anything we can pray for him over the next month. He pauses, then says that today his family found out that his dad has some serious health issues. I tell him we will pray about his family's situation. He asks, "Right now?" He catches me by surprise, but I answer, "Sure."

We all join hands around the table, and Jeremy is a part of our circle. He gets down on his knees as I pray for his dad. It is powerful!

Jeremy leaves to turn in our orders, and I am still a little shocked. I exclaim to the group, "Whoa! I have never seen that before." I don't know if I am more impressed with God for bringing Jeremy across our paths or with Jeremy for taking our offer to pray so seriously and not being hindered from joining us in prayer. He must have been hurting so much. God is so good!

Divine Appointment Principle #52:
*Do not be ashamed of our all-powerful God and be willing to go where He leads.*

# CHAPTER 59

# "WOULD YOU PRAY FOR ME?"

**A** friend and I are eating at a restaurant near her home in New Hampshire. We see each other only once in a great while, so we are having an enjoyable time catching up. Our waitress takes our order and then asks if there is anything else we want. When I ask her if there is anything we can pray for her over the next month, she encourages us to pray for her mother-in-law since her mother-in-law is already a Christian. I said that we will, but I am thinking that this is a rather strange response to my question.

When she returns to our table, I check again to see if there is anything that we can be praying for her; she sharply says, "No." We accept that response, and we begin eating our meal.

About 20 minutes later, another waitress comes up to our table and asks, "Would you pray for me?" We tell her that we would be happy to do so, and she gives us her request.

As she turns to leave our table, I ask her, "How did you know that we would pray for you?"

She relates how our waitress was back in the kitchen area complaining that her customers were trying to cram their religion down her throat. She adds, "You need to pray for her. I asked her if I could share her prayer request with you, and she wouldn't allow me to do so. She needs your prayers. This is her last night of working at this restaurant."

God is so good. I can't tell you how many times God has to remind me that I only see the outside, and He sees the inside. He knows for whom we need to be interceding.

Divine Appointment Principle #53:
*Even divine appointments who are opposed to God and who reject us can be used by God. Don't be discouraged.*

# CHAPTER 60

# WRONG MICHAEL AND SUSAN!

**W**e moved into our current subdivision in 1992. One of the first things Bonnie and I observed was a woman who was out walking every day. We commented how this woman was the most visible person in our subdivision.

I was out jogging one day when I noticed this same woman walking ahead of me. She had stopped and was talking with a gentleman on his front step. I heard him say to her that if Michael needed any help coaching this year, he was available. That registered in my mind as, Michael is her husband's name. I caught up to her eventually and walked beside her for a few moments. I started the conversation by remarking, "You are the most visible person in this subdivision. My wife and I are always looking for something to pray for people. Is there something in your life that we can be praying for you?"

Without any hesitation, she answered, "Peace!"

I said, "Fine. We will pray for peace."

I started to run off, then stopped and turned around to ask, "What is your first name?"

She replied, "Susan."

When I finished my jog, I looked up in our subdivision directory and went all the way through it to find a Michael and Susan. There was one household with those first names, and they lived on Nakoma Street. Their house was about a half mile from ours.

So I began praying each Monday for Michael and Susan. I would see Susan every once in a while when I was out jogging. We would say "Hi," but that was about the extent of our conversation. It must have been at least three years later that Susan was walking by our house one day, and I was prompted to ask her if she lived in our subdivision; she said no.

I thought to myself, "What? I have been praying for Michael and Susan on Nakoma Street for years, and it wasn't even the right couple." I discovered shortly afterward that this Michael and Susan lived in a subdivision a mile or so from our house. As a result, I started praying for both couples every Monday.

Now I was curious about Michael and Susan on Nakoma Street. Who were these people, and why would God trick me into praying for them each week? I simply continued to intercede for both couples weekly because I never felt the release from God to stop praying for either couple.

I had been interceding for both couples for fifteen years, when one morning I was jogging by Michael and Susan's house on Nakoma Street and noticed a gentleman in the driveway getting something out of the trunk of his car. I thought that this was my opportunity, so I walked up the driveway and asked, "Are you Michael?"

He assured me he was. I explained to him that I also lived in the subdivision, and God had tricked me into praying for him and his wife for the last fifteen years.

I asked him, "Why would God do that?"

He paused for a moment, then responded, "My wife and I went through a divorce a few years ago. Maybe that was why."

I said, "Yeah, maybe. I'll keep praying."

As I left his driveway, I thought about the incredible God we serve! I had never met this Michael and Susan, but God had me interceding for them at a difficult time in their lives.

To this day, I still intercede for both couples. I don't know what God is "up to," but I still do not have the freedom to take either of them off my Monday prayer list. I love the way God works!

Divine Appointment Principle #54:
*It is okay to pray for the "wrong" person. God knows what He is doing.*

# CHAPTER 61

# WRONG SEAT

This story is from my book entitled, *The Path Toward Passion,* Prayershop Publishing 2009. It bears repeating.

I am flying home from Manchester, New Hampshire, one Thursday morning. I have a connecting flight in Pittsburgh. I had prayed that morning that God would give me a special divine appointment that day.

I sit next to a gentleman from Toronto on the flight to Pittsburgh. I ask him for a prayer request, and he gives me one, but it wasn't really a "special" divine appointment.

A staff member from Impact has told me that a friend of ours, Kathy, will also be flying to Lansing through Pittsburgh the same day. I bump into Kathy at the Pittsburgh airport, and we are on the same flight to Lansing. She is traveling with her three-month-old son, Zachary. I tell her that I will sit next to her and help her with Zachary. My seat is 3C, but her seat is near the rear of the plane.

As we arrive at our gate, I notice that the mayor of Lansing is also on our flight. When we board, I see that the mayor is sitting directly behind my assigned seat. I tell Kathy that I will join her in a minute, but I want to ask the mayor for a prayer request first. I stand in front of my assigned seat and lean over my chair to introduce myself to the mayor. I ask him for a prayer request, and he explains that all politicians need prayer. He never really gives me anything specific, but I commit to pray for him anyway. I join Kathy in the back of the small plane. On the boarding

175

side of the plane, each row has just one seat. On the other side of the aisle, there are two seats. Kathy is seated next to the window with Zachary on her lap, and I am seated next to the aisle. A gentleman is seated across the aisle.

Just before takeoff, a flight attendant stops at our row and tells Kathy that she cannot sit there with her son on her lap because only one air mask is available for that seat. She directs Kathy to move across the aisle, and the gentleman takes the seat formerly belonging to Kathy. As we chat, I ask him for a prayer request. He says that he actually has two. I answer, "Great, what is the first one?" He and his wife are looking to purchase a house in Lansing; I can pray for them to find one. I say that I can do that and ask what his second prayer request is. He says that he and his wife need to get more involved in their church. I remark that this is a great prayer request, and I ask him which church they attend; he says South Lansing Christian Church. I am amazed. That is the same church that Kathy and I attend. God is so amazing. He put three of us from the same church in the same row on this plane. I am a little curious that I didn't know him. I assume that since I often travel on weekends, leading seminars in churches, I do not have the opportunity to know everyone at my home church.

I am still a little puzzled that I have never seen him before, so I ask him how long he has been a Christian. He explains that he has never been baptized. I ask if he understands the purpose of baptism, and he wants to know more about it. I explain its purpose and encourage him to consider being baptized this coming Sunday; he commits to think about it.

On Friday I pray all day for Jim to take this step of faith. On Saturday, I pray the same prayer. On Sunday, I pray that

176

today will be the day that Jim takes this important step of faith. At the end of our second service, Jim and his wife, Kate, come forward together, and he is baptized. I am blown away. I have interceded for him for three days. I discover after the service that his wife, Kate, has been praying for him for eight years. Kate is the real intercessor; I am a short-timer. What amazes me most is that God put someone next to me on a plane who was ready to say "yes" to Jesus, and I was in the *wrong seat*. Our God is phenomenal!

Divine Appointment Principle #55:
*I can be in the wrong place, and God can still work super-naturally.*

# CHAPTER 62

# "YOU LIVE ON CHIPPEWA DRIVE?"

I am astounded at how God orchestrates divine appointments with my neighbors. He is so clever.

I am flying out of Lansing early one Friday morning on my way to Detroit, and then on to Ft. Myers to lead a seminar at First Christian Church. I begin chatting with my seatmate, Marilyn. She is on her way to her nephew's wedding. She works at Okemos High School, and she lives in Okemos. I state that I live in Okemos also. I ask her where she lives; she says Chippewa Drive.

Surprised, I question, "You live on Chippewa Drive? I live on Chippewa Drive!" As it turns out, we live three houses apart, and we have never met. God is so funny. It is as if he is saying, "If you won't meet your neighbors on your own, I will put them next to you on an airplane."

Another time, I am boarding a flight to Lansing. It is late in the boarding process, and my assigned seat is 3C. As I board, I feel the need to sit in 4C. There is no one in 4D, so I assume I will be sitting by myself. Before long, a passenger named Mark comes along and sits down in 4D.

When we start chatting, I discover that he lives in DeWitt and is looking for a church. I recommend a church in DeWitt at which a friend of mine is on staff. I tell him where I live, and we are having a good time conversing. Suddenly the passenger in 4B speaks up and addresses Mark, introducing himself as Matt. As it turns out, he had attended high school with Mark's younger brother. They exchange some information; then he turns to me and asks, "You live on Chippewa Drive?" I answer in the affirmative; he says that He does also. He describes the house, and I instantly know exactly where he lives, less than a quarter of a mile south of me. We have never met.

A third time, I am getting the mail one day, when I notice that one of the letters is addressed to one of my neighbors, but a different name is on the envelope. I decide to deliver it in person. Steve, whom I have not met before, answers the door. I explain that I have a letter addressed to Stephen L., and he says, "That's me." I hand him the letter and ask how long he has lived here. He says that it has been just two months. I tell him that I didn't even know the house had "exchanged hands." He says that he is a good friend with the previous owner's son. When he heard that they wanted to sell, he purchased the house directly from them without using a real estate company. (I guess I missed the moving vans also.)

I tell Steve that Bonnie and I are always looking for something in our neighbors' lives for which we can be praying. I ask if I can be praying for something for him personally. He responds, "My live-in girlfriend and I are getting married in two weeks. We are having the ceremony in the back yard, so you can be praying for a nice, sunny day." I tell him that I will be praying for great weather.

The wedding day arrives, and God provides a gorgeous Michigan summer day. I am excited for our new neighbor and his wife.

A year or two passes. I haven't seen Steve since our first meeting because He seldom works outside. It is Halloween, and we are prepared with a large bowl of candy for "trick or

180

treaters." The doorbell rings, and Bonnie answers it. It is Steve and his very young daughter. They chat for a minute before Bonnie calls to me and says that our neighbor Steve is at the door. She wants me to come and meet him. I decide to have some fun with him, so I come to the front door and say, "I already met him. He asked me to pray for good weather for his wedding ceremony in his back yard. He had an awesome day, and he never said, 'Thank you.'"

Steve laughs and says, "Oh, yeah, thanks." We have a good time catching up.

God is so good at orchestrating divine appointments with people who live on my street. Our God has a tremendous amount of ability in this area. Unfortunately, many Christians are not aware of God's creativity in orchestrating divine appointments with neighbors. As a result, they often miss great opportunities with the people who live around them.

Divine Appointment Principle #56:
*God knows how to provide divine appointments with those who live near us, even on airplanes or by delivering mail. He "connects" us to others so we can reach out to them.*

# CHAPTER 63

# "YOU MUST BE AN ANGEL"

**I** had rented a car and had driven to Iowa and Missouri to teach and to visit some donors to our ministry in a couple of places. Tired from spending several days on the road, I am now back in Michigan driving on I-94 near Benton Harbor. I stop at a Speedway® store along the expressway to fill up with gas.

As I am pumping gas, a vehicle pulls up on the other side of the gas pumps. A lady exits her car and begins pumping gas. She looks at my car and asks me how I like it. I explain to her that it is a rental, but I have enjoyed driving it on my five-day road trip.

She continues talking, and then it hits me; this is a divine appointment. I ask her for her first name, and she tells me it is Robin. I mention to her that I look for things to pray for others, and I ask if there is something in her life for which I can be praying. She responds, "You must be an angel. Please be praying for my father, Paul, because he is not doing well physically, and I have moved back home to care for him." She is so grateful for the opportunity to give me a prayer request.

We say our goodbyes, and I get back on eastbound I-94. This divine appointment has surprised me. As I drive toward Kalamazoo, I keep thinking, "God, only You could give me a divine appointment as I was pumping gas, and I didn't even initiate the conversation." As always, His timing was perfect.

Divine Appointment Principle #57:
*Divine appointments can happen anywhere and at any time. Just be alert and ready.*

# CHAPTER 64

# "YOU WANT TO EAT OUT?"

**B**onnie comes home from work one Tuesday and announces that she would like to eat at Applebee's® for dinner. I am not really interested in doing so. I do my best to change her mind. I suggest that we order pizza; she says no. I suggest that we eat at Big Boy® since she likes their desserts; again she says no. I plead for Mountain Jack's® since we have gift certificates there; she says no for the third time. (Why do I get the feeling that I am losing this discussion?) I finally relent, and we head off to Applebee's®.

The hostess seats us, and we begin to look over our menus. Our waitress, Heather, approaches our table and asks what she can get us to drink. We both want water, so she hurries off to fulfill our requests. She returns and asks what we want to eat. We give her our order, and then I asked her what we can pray for her.

She asks, "You want to pray for me?"

I say "Yes."

"Why do you want to pray for me?" she inquires.

"Because you are our waitress, and we assume you have something that we can pray for you," I reply.

"I can't believe that you want to pray for me," she says in bewilderment and disbelief.

"Why is that so hard for you to believe?" I ask.

185

She begins, "I am a senior at Michigan State University, and I will graduate in a couple of months. My whole time at MSU I have been into the party scene, but just a few weeks ago I decided that I need to stop wasting my time and find out who God is. And here you are sitting in my area of the restaurant asking for a prayer request. I can't believe you want to pray for me."

She disappears just long enough to turn in our order and returns, repeating her previous statement, "I can't believe you want to pray for me." She is still in shock; she simply cannot grasp how God could do something like this for her. Then she blurts out, "I don't care where you go to church; I want to go to your church."

Now I am the one to be impressed with God. Bonnie knew we needed to be at Applebee's® that night, and God arranged an amazing divine appointment with Heather. Our God is phenomenal!

On the way home, I apologize to Bonnie for my resistance to eating at Applebee's®. Now I realize that spouses can really abuse this idea of eating out, but sometimes God will draw us to a place and expect us to simply show up and wait to see what He does.

Two weeks later, Heather is sitting next to us in church. We can trust that God knows exactly what He is doing. The question is, "Will we follow Him?"

Divine Appointment Principle #58:
*When God is leading us somewhere we don't want to go, go anyway. He often has a divine appointment waiting.*

CONCLUSION

# WHERE DO I GO FROM HERE?

**I** have concluded that I always need to be ready for God's next divine appointment. I never know who it will be or when it will occur, but I do know that the next divine appointment will happen soon. The question is, "Will I be ready?" Think of the number of people who could be impacted for the Kingdom through "God-orchestrated" divine appointments if we would intentionally seek to recognize them and follow God's leading. It is up to you and me to "see" what God is doing right in front of us. After all, they are God's divine appointments.

Please take the following question to heart.

*What divine appointment does God have waiting for you, and what response will you make to His prompting?*

# HOW YOU CAN USE THIS BOOK

You can use this book in a variety of ways. The primary objective of this book is to show people how to glorify God through divine appointments. When you put the divine appointment principles in this book into practice, God will be greatly glorified with your life.

**1.** *Personal Study:* You can personally use this book to help you be more aware of God's divine appointments in your everyday life. As you deepen your intimacy with God, He will use divine appointments as one way to affirm His presence in your life.

**2.** *Mentoring, Discipling, or Coaching:* If you are investing your life into the life of another through mentoring, discipling, or coaching, you can use this book to help him/her become more aware of divine appointments and what God is doing. Obedience is a key factor for maturing in Jesus. Many of God's divine appointments require obedience on our part.

**3.** *Small Groups:* Your small group would greatly benefit by examining several divine appointment principles each week in order to solidify the concepts in their daily lives. God can open missional opportunities for your small group in your community through divine appointments. It will be very encouraging to your small group to share what divine appointments God is providing each week.

Regardless of how you use this book, may God use you in wild and creative ways to bring glory to Him.

If you have a special divine appointment I encourage you to share it with me so we can both be emboldened and inspired. You can send your divine appointment story to me by e-mail to dtrune@iimin.org or dtrune@gmail.com.

If you recognized yourself in any of these stories, please update me on what God is doing in your life.

APPENDIX

# DIVINE APPOINTMENT PRINCIPLES

Here is a summary of the divine appointment principles that I have shared with you over the last 58 chapters. These are good reminders for me to review often. Our God is always at work, and He is unstoppable.

1. God loves to surprise us with a clear demonstration of His power. Expect it.

2. I must be ready to instantly respond to where God is leading. Be flexible.

3. Our God has a real sense of humor. He shows us that side of Himself so we can laugh with Him.

4. When God abruptly changes your plans, expect a divine appointment.

5. In the midst of a temptation to respond emotionally, look for God's bigger picture.

6. God has the ability to make things exciting even when I am bored.

7. God is even more interested than we are in having people read His Word.

8. Sometimes I want to rest but God wants me to bless others through a divine appointment. I can trust Him to know and take care of my needs.

9. Some divine appointments are routine. Others are amazingly wild. Go with what God orchestrates.

10. God will work far beyond my own self-serving desires.

11. People don't need our judgment; they need our prayers.

12. I need to simply obey, regardless if it makes sense to me at the moment.

13. God can lead me to anyone at anytime because He knows exactly where he or she is at the moment.

14. My perceived purpose for being in a place may be totally different from God's actual purpose.

15. Don't say "No" for other people. Ask the question anyway. God may open an amazing, unexpected door.

16. God can interrupt our schedule at any time He chooses, and He may be testing our willingness to obey His prompting.

17. God often expects us to show boldness, but He always expects us to show love.

18. God's orchestrating is split-second perfect.

19. Finding a needle in a haystack is an everyday occurrence for God.

20. God can affirm what I am doing through a divine appointment even when I am not looking for it.

21. When God's people show up with generosity and with love, the world will want to know why.

22. In my panic, God doesn't.

23. Some divine appointments are searching for something that we have, if only we will take the time to share it.

24. Some divine appointments are too obvious to miss.

25. Auto accidents are great places for finding divine appointments. Be a blessing.

26. It is not about your divine appointment's faith in God; it is all about yours.

27. Don't be afraid to let God prove Himself.

28. God knows how to grant us favor with divine appointments from other ministries (even ahead of time).

29. God knows how to use us to affirm others' obedience.

30. God knows how to use divine appointments to teach us character and humility.

31. God will bring divine appointments into our lives at critical moments in their lives.

32. Sometimes God provides a second chance at a divine appointment when we miss the first one.

33. Sometimes we have to probe beneath the surface to discover the real need to be praying for in a divine appointment's life.

34. God knows how to connect some divine appointments with my friends in order for Him to receive the greatest glory.

35. Some divine appointments look fine on the outside but are hurting deeply on the inside. We need to care enough to ask for a prayer request.

36. If we are serious about interceding for a group of people, God can orchestrate a divine appointment with someone from that group. He is amazing.

37. Not everyone will respond well to being a divine appointment. That is no reason to stop looking for them.

38. When people are experiencing overwhelming sorrow and distress, God sends intercessors to love them and pray for them in their moment of greatest need.

39. No one is outside of God's reach. Just love them unconditionally.

40. In spite of me not being at my best, God can still work supernaturally through me. It is all about His abilities, not mine.

41. We can even pray divine appointments into existence.

42. God knows the best way to present truth to our divine appointments.

43. If I focus on my needs and desires, I will typically miss great divine appointments.

44. Pray for our divine appointments to be "right" with God.

45. God can be specifically preparing us for a divine appointment several days in advance. Our responsibility is to be prepared.

46. God will give the right question to ask our divine appointment. Just listen.

47. When I find myself hanging out with a stranger, I can assume that it is a divine appointment.

48. When divine appointments see God move supernaturally, they will want to share it with others. God is so powerful!

49. God knows how to connect us to others in a divine appointment in order to provide a "bridge" for them to return to Him.

50. Sometimes God will effortlessly use a divine appointment to pave the way to a second divine appointment.

51. Don't underestimate how deeply God can impact a divine appointment's heart by being asked for a prayer request.

52. Do not be ashamed of our all-powerful God and be willing to go where He leads.

53. Even divine appointments who are opposed to God and who reject us can be used by God. Don't be discouraged.

54. It is okay to pray for the wrong person. God knows what He is doing.

55. I can be in the wrong place, and God can still work supernaturally.

56. God knows how to provide divine appointments with those who live near us, even on airplanes or by delivering mail. He "connects" us to others so we can reach out to them.

57. Divine appointments can happen anywhere and at any time. Just be alert and ready.

58. When God is leading us somewhere we don't want to go, go anyway. He often has a divine appointment waiting.

*You can download a PDF file of these principles from www.deantrune.com.*

# THE AUTHOR

Dean Trune grew up in a Christian home on a farm in rural Michigan. After college, he began working for AC Spark Plug®, which was a division of General Motors Corporation®. At the age of 34, God called him out of engineering and into campus ministry at Michigan State University. After 11 years at MSU, God again called him to begin a prayer-based campus ministry organization and to begin speaking nationally and internationally about going deeper with God.

Today Dean lives in Okemos, Michigan, with his wife, Bonnie. They have two adult children and two grandsons. The picture of his family of the back cover shows Ryan, Reka, and little Zane (second grandson) on the left and Kim and DeShawn (first grandson) on the right. He is extremely proud of his family.

Dean continues to lead Intentional Impact and to speak in churches, on campuses, and for retreats and conferences about this incredible relationship with God that is available to all. Dean is a certified life coach, and he coaches many people in ministry around the country, encouraging and challenging them as they deepen their relationship with God.

If you would like more information about Dean's ministry or the resources available, you can go to either www.iimin.org or www.deantrune.com. You are welcome to e-mail him at dtrune@gmail.com. His blog is available on the web sites. He is a fellow pursuer of God and an ardent believer that this relationship with God is rather simple; either God leads or we lead.